MAKING FRIENDS

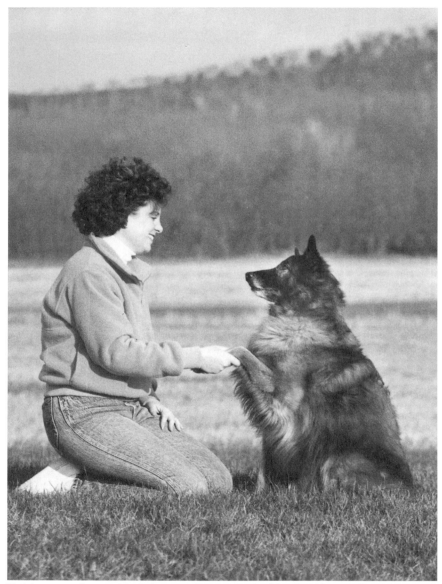

Training your dog positively is a good way to make friends with your dog.

MAKING FRIENDS

Training Your Dog Positively

LINDA COLFLESH

HOWELL
BOOK
HOUSE

This book is printed on acid-free paper. ∞

Copyright © 1990, 2004 by Howell Book House. All rights reserved

Drawings on pp. 25 and 112 by Deb Mickey; photos on pp. 187 and 192 (top) by Sharon Sakson. All remaining photos © Brad Wood

Howell Book House
Published by Wiley Publishing, Inc., Hoboken, New Jersey
Published simultaneously in Canada

For general information about our other products and services, please contact our Customer Care Department within the United States at (800) 762-2974, outside the United States at (317) 572-3993 or fax (317) 572-4002.

Wiley also publishes its books in a variety of electronic formats. Some content that appears in print may not be available in electronic books. For more information about Wiley products, visit our web site at www.wiley.com.

Library of Congress Cataloging-in-Publication Data:

Colflesh, Linda.
  Making friends : training your dog positively / by Linda Colflesh ; photos by Brad Wood.
    p. cm.
  ISBN 0-7645-7329-2 (alk. paper)
  1. Dogs—Training. I. Title.
  SF431.C58 2004
  636.7'0887—dc22
                              2004014595

Printed in the United States of America

10 9 8 7 6 5 4 3 2 1

To my mother and father
To Shauna and Carla, my first dogs
To Quest, who taught me so much
To Brad, my husband

Thank you for the love to grow on.

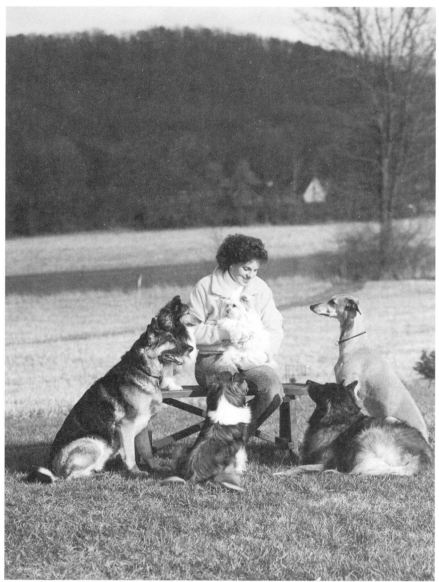

The author surrounded by some of her friends.

Contents

Acknowledgments

This book would not have been possible without the support of my husband, Bradford J. Wood, M.D. Brad provided me with a never-ending supply of patience and emotional and financial support. In spite of having very limited free time because of his work as a family physician, he gave it up without complaint to take the photographs for the book. He is truly "the wind beneath my wings."

A special thank you must go to my good friend, Nancy Heckman. She proofread the entire first manuscript and the parts I rewrote for this book. When I needed to talk about my writing, Nancy patiently listened on our many dog walks together. Our dog walks keep me sane!

Because I wanted a variety of dogs in the pictures for this book, I had to ask for the help of many friends to pose for them. I want to thank all of them and their cooperative dogs for their time and patience. I especially want to thank the members of the Carlisle Dog Club, who were all very supportive. I also want to thank all of my students and their dogs from whom I have learned what I shared with you in this book.

As I have worked on the changes for this *Making Friends*, my beautiful, faithful Irish Setter, Kyra, has always been lying right beside my chair. Now, that's a friend.

Making Friends could not have been written without the help of many friends, both canine and human. Thank you to all of them!

It's best to begin training when your puppy is 9 to 12 weeks old.

MAKING FRIENDS

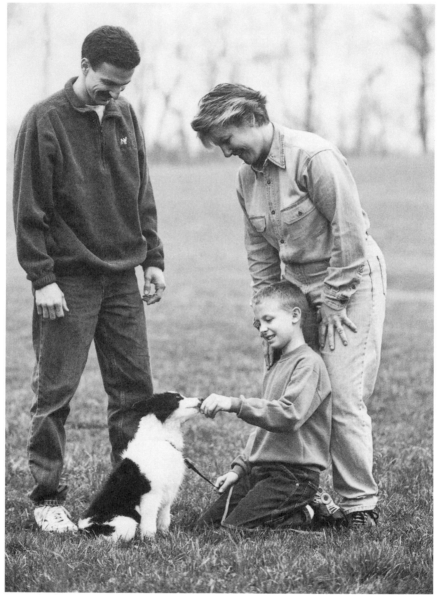
A good relationship with your dog is based on understanding and positive training.

1

Good Relationships Are Built on Good Training

As a dog obedience instructor, I see many dog owners who are having problems with their dogs. Their dogs won't come when called, they drag their owners down the street when walked on leash, they jump up on company, they chew on furniture, and they urinate on the carpets. These owners are frustrated and confused by their dogs. Some are very angry. Even though the owners and dogs love each other, they do not understand each other. Both are unhappy.

At least the owners and dogs I see as an obedience instructor are getting help. As a volunteer worker at an SPCA shelter, I have seen the dissolution of many poor dog-owner relationships—death for the dog. Millions of dogs are euthanized every year in the United States. While overpopulation is a part of the problem, many dogs are disposed of by their owners because of behavior problems that could have been solved with good training. I hope through this book to prevent some of these deaths.

I have been teaching dog obedience for 28 years. I got started by taking my first dog, Shauna, an Irish Setter, to a dog obedience class. We weren't having any problems; it just seemed like a fun thing to do. The obedience training allowed us to do a lot more things together. I could take her to my college classes because she would lie down and stay for 50 minutes. (She had to be very good because dogs weren't supposed to be in the college buildings.) She would ride quietly in the elevator. We could play Frisbee because she would come when called. Best of all, the obedience training helped Shauna and me cope with her timidity, which was the result of poor breeding. When we finished the class, we were awarded a ribbon for being the most improved. At the time I didn't stop to think that being most improved probably meant that we were the worst at the beginning of the class. I was thrilled and decided to pursue an American Kennel Club (AKC) obedience title.

After a lot more work, I showed Shauna in obedience competition. At our second show, we won first place in our class and a big trophy. Now I was really hooked. I continued showing, joined an obedience training club, and was asked to help teach classes. My husband was in medical school and gone a lot of the time, so teaching obedience classes seemed a good way to spend evenings. I discovered that I liked helping people solve their problems with their dogs and was good at it. It was tremendously satisfying to help an owner who came into class threatening to take his dog to the SPCA if things did not improve and left the class pleased with his dog's behavior.

Over the years, I continued to learn about dogs and dog training. I learned by experience, by reading everything I could find on dogs, and by attending many dog training seminars. My best teachers were my dogs. Besides my Irish Setter, I had a Borzoi (also known as a Russian Wolfhound) and a Greyhound. I learned so much from them. I currently have another Irish Setter. (You can see I don't choose easy-to-train breeds.) My husband is training his third Belgian Tervuren. The fact that a busy family physician could put multiple titles on his dogs tends to discourage arguments from my dog training students that they don't have time to train their dogs. While we enjoy the challenge of showing our dogs, our primary enjoyment of them is their companionship. I am just as proud of the way they behave at my parents' home when the family gathers for holidays as I am of any show ring performance.

I want to help you develop a good relationship with your dog by teaching you to train and understand your dog. My relationships with my dogs over the years have greatly enriched my life. I want to share what I've learned about training dogs so that you, too, can experience the joys of sharing your life with a dog.

Good Relationships Are Built on Realistic Expectations

It is regrettable how many times I have had conversations that went something like this:

> New puppy owner: "My husband and I just bought two Siberian Husky puppies. I think they need some training."
> Me: "Are they housebroken?"
> New puppy owner: "No. They go all over the house."
> Me: "What have you done to housebreak them?"
> New puppy owner: "Well, nothing really."
> Me: "Do you have a fenced yard?"
> New puppy owner: "No."

Me: "How do you plan to exercise them?"

New puppy owner: "I guess we'll just train them to stay in the yard."

Me: "Do you know how hard it is to train one, let alone *two* Siberian Huskies to stay in an unfenced yard? Siberians are known for their independent nature and urge to run."

New puppy owner: "Well, if we can't train them soon, we won't be able to keep them. Will this take more than a few lessons?"

What do you think the chances are for these puppies' futures?

Many dog-owner relationships are the victims of unrealistic expectations. Some of these expectations are caused by what we see on television, some are caused by selective memories of childhood, dogs, and others are caused by not realizing that all dogs are different.

Dog ownership looks so easy on television. That myth has been perpetuated by TV shows and dog food commercials. According to TV, you give the dog a little love, throw some dog food at him once a day, and *voilà*—he turns into a completely obedient pet who would gladly give his life to protect his family. My favorites are commercials that show an adorable little child being mobbed by a litter of cute puppies. In reality, puppies of that age are armed with little needles for teeth that send children screaming for their mothers when their arms are punctured. And have you ever seen a dog on TV on leash? No. TV dogs, unlike those in the real world, all immediately come when called. This would all be amusing if the fact of the matter were not that when dogs do not live up to these TV myths, the dog often gets blamed and is disposed of.

People frequently get a dog because a friend or neighbor has one who is wonderful. These people go out and get the same breed, but then are surprised when their dog is different. They are unaware of the great differences in the personalities of dogs of the same breed. Perhaps the neighbor's dog came from a good breeder, while they got theirs from a pet shop. Many of the puppies sold in pet shops are the result of indiscriminate breeding with total disregard for temperament. People also ignore the differences age will make in a dog's behavior, wondering why their eight-month-old Labrador Retriever is a terror, while the eight-year-old Lab down the street is a placid, sweet dog.

I recently was consulted by the owners of a Golden Retriever who could not get over how different the behavior of their dog was from that of the dog's father, who lived down the street. Of course, there was an age difference. Their Golden, Chadley, was just a little more than one year old; his father, Max, was five years old. I explained the behavior differences that this age difference would cause, but they were still doubtful.

One of their major complaints about Chadley was that he jumped up on the kids. The kids didn't like Chadley (which was a reflection of their mother's feelings), but they loved to play with Max. Max never jumped up on them. That's when a little warning bell went off in my head. A Golden

Retriever who never jumped up when kids played with him? Either he was an *extremely* well-trained dog, or, I asked, "Is Max a little overweight?" Bingo! Max was a two-ton tank. He *couldn't* jump up! This "little" difference never occurred to poor Chadley's owners. A little more checking revealed that Max, the supposed saint of dogdom, had stolen a whole chocolate cake from the kitchen counter recently. Max's owners just laughed about it, but when Chadley did the same kind of thing, his owners considered getting rid of him.

People also ignore the differences environment can make in a dog's behavior. The German Shepherd down the street may behave better than yours because his owner is home all day, gives him more exercise, has taken him to obedience training classes, or has a quieter, less stressful household. Dogs today live in a difficult environment. Often both adult members of a household, if there even are two, work outside the home, leaving the dog home all day alone and bored. When I hear an owner complain, "But my old Cocker Spaniel, Buffy, that we had when I was a kid never chewed on the furniture," I remind the owner that Buffy was probably rarely left home alone, could get plenty of exercise running loose around the neighborhood, had other dogs and kids to play with, and was an old dog.

Having realistic expectations of your dog will help you anticipate and solve problems. Your dog is a dog and has needs. He needs exercise, company, mental stimulation, and to be taught the rules of the society he lives in. He needs to be forgiven for acting like a dog, even if that is not the way you want him to act.

Is it ever possible to have your own super dog? Yes, with the right dog, the right care, and *the right training*.

Choosing a Training Method

There are many different ways to train a dog. Of course, you want to choose a method that is easy and effective. However, there should be a more important consideration: the method's effect on your relationship with your dog. A good relationship is based on respect for one another's feelings, so the training method you choose should be one that respects your dog's intelligence and dignity and is as gentle and pleasant as possible.

To help choose a method, try to look at training from your dog's point of view. Imagine that you suddenly find yourself on another planet with beings that don't look or act like you (which is the position your dog is in). You don't understand a word of their language (just like an untrained dog doesn't understand English). You want to fit in somehow and get along with these beings. A being who is significantly bigger than you puts a choke collar around your neck, attaches a leash and pulls on it, giving you the command "zork." You aren't thrilled about the collar and leash, but you get up and start walking along behind the Big Thing. Suddenly he yells, "Zork!" and jerks you forward on the leash. You don't know what you've done wrong, but he seems to want you to walk ahead of him, so that's where you continue walking. This time, he roars, "No, *Zork!*" and gives you a hard jerk backward. Now you're really confused. You don't know where he wants you to walk. After several more painful jerks, you finally figure out that the only place you can walk and not have him jerk you is on his left side. You've learned what "zork" means, but you're not very anxious to learn more—at least not that way.

Let's try another scenario. You are again helplessly stranded on the planet of Big Things. One of the Big Things comes up to you and shows you that he has a handful of things that look remarkably like candy. He holds one close to your nose so you can sniff it. It smells like candy. You're a little hungry, so when he hands you one, you eat it. Wow, they're great! Big Thing takes a few steps away and says, "Zork," all the while holding out the hand with the candy. You take a few steps to follow him, and he hands you another piece. This time when he says, "Zork!" and walks away, you are quicker to follow him. Again you get another piece. You walk along together, with you respectively a little behind him. He repeats, "Zork!" in an inviting tone of voice and lures you forward to his left side with the hand holding the candy. When you get right alongside him, he gives you another piece. You've got it! You get a reward if you walk on his left side when he says, "Zork." You can't wait for the next lesson to begin.

The second training example illustrates the use of positive reinforcement. My system of training is based on positive reinforcement, mostly in the form of food rewards. But that isn't the way I've always trained. Everything I read and heard cautioned against using food to train a dog. Then I had a difficult training problem. I wanted to train my Borzoi, Carla, to retrieve. Carla was a beautiful, elegant dog who only did AKC obedience competition to humor me. We had completed her Companion Dog (CD) AKC obedience title. I wanted to try for the next title, the Companion Dog Excellent (CDX), but there was one problem. A dog is required to retrieve to get this title. Carla had never shown any interest in retrieving anything except food from the kitchen counter. I had previously trained my first dog, an Irish Setter, to retrieve reliably for the show ring, but I was uncomfortable with the way I had done it. The method I had used was based on applying force with the choke collar. At the time it was considered a humane method of teaching the retrieve because the more popular method was to pinch the dog's ear. Nevertheless, it didn't seem the right thing to do morally, causing a dog so much discomfort just to get an AKC obedience title that meant nothing to the dog.

Then I read an article in a dog training magazine about training a dog to retrieve using food. Although I had always been told that you should never use food to train a dog, I was desperate. I decided to try it, and it worked beautifully! Carla got her CDX title easily, and I learned that you *can* train a dog with food.

The Advantages of Using Food to Train Your Dog

Training with food is a better way to train dogs. It is easier, more effective, and certainly a lot more fun for you and your dog. Since I trained dogs for many years without using food, I have a good basis for comparison.

Training consists of two parts: communicating to your dog what you want, and motivating your dog to do it. Food can help with both. But before you can start, you need to get his attention. Without it, training is impossible. Using food gives you an easy way to get your dog's attention. You have something he wants, so he will be anxious to learn how to get it.

Teaching a dog to lie down is a good example of how food works well for communicating what you want. Let's say you want to train your full-grown Great Dane, Lyndy, to lie down. You could try to pull her down with the leash. If she decides to resist, and she probably will since it is instinctive for a dog to brace against the force of something pulling on her, you're in for quite a battle. Alternatively, you could lift her front legs when she is sitting and gradually ease her down. Unfortunately, the only thing Lyndy may learn from this is to allow herself to be lifted down, while you get a sore back. Dogs often do not understand that you want them to make a motion on their own, even after you have helped them do that motion many times.

An easier way would be to use food. Attach it to your dog's nose like a magnet, and slowly draw her down to the floor. *Voilà!* Easy, huh? And the motion you make with your hand becomes a hand signal when you no longer need the food in your hand.

The second part of training—motivating your dog to do what you want—involves making a choice. You can make your dog do what you want out of fear of punishment, or you can make your dog work to earn a reward. The use of food to motivate your dog utilizes the psychological principle of positive reinforcement. Positive reinforcement is part of a larger theory of learning known as behavior modification. Basically, the principle of positive reinforcement says that positive reinforcement increases the probability that the behavior preceding it will occur again. For example, if you call your dog and he gets a treat when he comes, he is more likely to come the next time you call. In less fancy terminology, a positive reinforcement is a reward.

While there are many types of rewards for dogs, food is convenient and easy to use, can be given in small amounts, can function as a magnet to draw a dog into a desired position, and is appealing to a wide variety of dogs. It is good for dogs of all ages, from bouncy seven-week-old puppies, to unruly adolescents, to set-in-their-ways adult dogs, to fragile old dogs. Food works well for all breeds, from the eager-to-please Golden Retriever to the difficult-to-persuade Chow Chow. It also works for mixed breeds, and for dogs of all personalities. Food is a good tool to build the confidence of shy dogs and to work with aggressive dogs.

Trying to force Lyndy down.

An easier way to train, using a food lure. (Great Dane)

Using food as a training tool does not require athletic strength or coordination. Because of this it is an ideal method for children, older people, or someone who has physical limitations. And while timing is important in the successful use of food, bad timing of food delivery is not going to cause the problems that bad timing of force causes.

One advantage of training with food is that a child can train a big dog. (German Shepherd)

Other Rewards

There are other rewards in addition to food. A reward, or positive reinforcement, is anything the dog is willing to work to earn. Rewards other than food can be a tennis ball or favorite toy, freedom to explore a new environment, a chasing or wrestling game with the owner, an opportunity to play with other dogs, and praise.

Praise is the only reward utilized in many methods of dog training. In reality, praise functions as a very weak reward for most dogs. Trainers who are disdainful of the use of food often assert proudly that their dogs work for praise, implying that their training is superior because their dogs work out of love. However, these trainers are combining praise with strong collar corrections. A good example would be the traditional way of training a dog to heel, which is walking on the handler's left side without pulling on the leash. The dog is commanded to heel, then given jerks on the leash whenever he moves out of the desired position. (Does this sound familiar?) He is then praised when he is back in position. After repetition, the dog responds to the heel command without the leash being jerked, and is praised when he does so. At this point it appears that the dog is working to earn praise. What is really happening is that the dog is working to avoid being jerked on the leash.

Nonetheless, praise is a necessary part of dog training the positive way. Praise strengthens the social bond between dog and trainer. It enables the dog to tell what the trainer is feeling. The dog is accustomed to "reading" his

owner's mood by observing his body language and listening to his tone of voice. (Hopefully, you will soon be able to read your dog's body language as well as he reads yours.) The dog needs the reassurance verbal praise provides. The dog is routinely talked to in his daily life with his owner and would be stressed by a sudden silence during training. It's easy to forget to praise your dog when you are also giving food rewards. Actually, you should always praise your dog *before* giving him his food reward. When you do this, the praise takes on the rewarding properties of the food. The praise becomes a "conditioned reinforcer." A conditioned reinforcer is something that is initially meaningless, such as the words "good dog" are to a dog, but through association with an already established reward, the conditioned reinforcer becomes rewarding. Most dogs learn the meaning of "good dog" through unintentional training on the part of the owner. The dog makes an association between the words "good dog" and being petted by a happy owner. With a conditioned reinforcer, you can reward the dog when you don't have food and you can reward behaviors when the dog is away from you and you can't give him food. So praise has two roles: as a conditioned reinforcer, and as reassurance.

You may be worried about your dog's behavior being dependent on the food rewards—that he won't obey your commands unless you have food in your hands. While this is a real concern, I'll show you how to prevent this from happening by using the food properly in training, then gradually reducing your dog's dependence on it.

The Disadvantages of Using Force to Train Your Dog

What happens if you don't use positive reinforcement to train your dog? You'll have to rely more on force, which has many disadvantages. Not the least of these is that people dislike using force on their dogs. It is unfortunate that some dogs never get trained because owners who have been exposed to training based mainly on force, and don't like it, ultimately give up on dog training altogether, wrongly assuming that all training is done the same way. Their dogs are then doomed to live in a household where the owner cannot effectively communicate with them. The natural resistance of some dog owners to cause their dogs pain or discomfort is often looked upon by other dog trainers as a lack of character on the part of the new dog trainer. I'll never forget sitting at a seminar for dog obedience instructors and listening to the lecturer saying thankfully, "Trainers become less squeamish as they go along." While using force to train a dog is necessary at times, no one should be forced to lose their inhibitions against causing their dog discomfort.

A major disadvantage of force is that it does not tell a dog what to do, only what *not* to do. A classic example of this problem is seen when people attempt to housebreak a dog by using punishment. The dog is punished whenever he relieves himself in the house. Sometimes what the dog figures out is that in order to avoid punishment, he should be careful not to relieve himself in the presence of his owner. Instead, he will wait until he can get away from his owner to relieve himself in another room or behind the sofa. Taken to extremes, this can result in a dog who will not relieve himself outside when walked on leash because his owner is present. After a lot of suffering, these dogs often end up dead at a Humane Society facility because they supposedly couldn't be housebroken.

Another disadvantage of relying on force to train a dog is that after receiving many small punishments for not performing properly while being trained, the dog reacts by trying to avoid the training situation or even the trainer altogether. Because punishment doesn't let the dog know what the owner wants, the dog may not know how to stop the punishment. When this happens, the dog can develop a sense of helplessness and become depressed or neurotic. Eventually the owner's relationship with his dog may deteriorate to the point where the dog avoids him.

This happens with many dogs who come to me for help after their owners have taken an obedience class in which training is based on force. When the training leash and collar come out, the dog tries to hide or run away. One woman had the frightening experience of having her dog run away in the middle of an obedience class that was being held outdoors under lights after dark. After 45 terror-filled minutes of searching by driving through fields with her car, she found her dog huddled against a fence, equally frightened.

A dog with a more assertive personality may bite to stop the punishment. One student in a class of mine had that happen to him when trying to teach his German Shepherd, Kahn, to stand on command. I saw Jim give Kahn a command to stand, but he pulled upward on the collar, which was the signal to sit. Kahn, a handsome dog of good temperament, was confused and didn't stand. I explained to Jim what he was doing, but he ignored me. While I was busy with someone else, Jim lost his temper and got rough with Kahn because he was not standing. After a warning growl, Kahn bit Jim—not hard enough to break the skin, but enough to get his point across.

Another disadvantage of force is that often the dog only obeys when on leash. If a dog is trained to obey in order to avoid being jerked on the leash, once the leash is removed, the dog's motivation to perform is gone, and so is his training.

A skillful trainer with the right dog may be able to use force without incurring the disadvantages we have just discussed. However, beginner trainers are not skillful, and we don't all have the dogs with the right temperaments for this kind of training. Since there is an easier, kinder way to train a dog, why not use it?

The Role of Force in Positive Training

In spite of its disadvantages, force may sometimes be necessary when training your dog. Force can be as gentle as lightly restraining a nine-week-old puppy with your hands to teach him to stay. In fact, you are using a very mild form of force whenever you restrain your dog on a leash in order to keep him with you during training. Looked at this way, force is an unavoidable part of training. In training the positive way, you will minimize the use of force, but you will have to use it sometimes. Used in the context of training based on positive reinforcement, the negative effects of force are for the most part minimal.

The amount of force you'll have to use depends on many factors, such as the individual personality of your dog, your dog's age when you are starting training, and what you want to accomplish. For instance, a submissive dog of quiet temperament who rarely leaves her house and fenced backyard and started training at 12 weeks of age will need a minimum of force in her training. On the other hand, a large, rambunctious male dog who is just starting training at a year of age, doesn't get enough exercise, and has to be walked on leash in a busy neighborhood will probably need more force.

The situations in which force is useful often involve distractions. If something attracts a dog more than the food, praise, or play you can offer, your dog will be distracted. If playing outside on a nice day is more attractive to your dog than the treat he'll get when he comes inside, he won't come in when you call him unless you force him to. If your compulsively friendly Golden Retriever wants to jump on your elderly aunt more than he wants to earn a reward by sitting, forcing him not to jump up is definitely a good idea. However, force should be used only *after* the dog has been trained and you are 100 percent sure he understands what you want.

The use of force in training should not be confused with anger. Trust is an important part of a good relationship with a dog. The fastest way to lose a dog's trust is to let anger get in the way of good training. Anger is usually the result of wrongly blaming your dog for something you dislike or having unrealistic expectations.

To build a good relationship, you have to stop blaming your dog for acting like a dog—for jumping up to greet people, for running away to chase a squirrel, or for relieving his anxiety when he is left home alone by destructive chewing. Destructive behavior while an owner is away is the circumstance that probably triggers the most anger in dog owners. Any group of dog owners can exchange stories of havoc wreaked in their absence: couches chewed to a pulp, irreplaceable molding around windows destroyed, wall-to-wall diarrhea. The list is endless. One of the most memorable I've experienced with my own dogs was returning home to find that our young Belgian Tervuren, Sabre, had pulled a *large* plant out of its pot and then played in the dirt—on our white carpet!

Did we punish him? No! Punishing Sabre would have accomplished nothing other than providing an outlet for our frustration. I'm sure he saw no difference between our indoor plant and the sticks he played with outside. There is no way he could have understood that we were punishing him for something he probably did hours before, so it would have not prevented a future occurrence. I'm sure that if we had yelled at him and acted angry, Sabre would have acted afraid of us. Many people mistakenly interpret this fearful, submissive behavior as the dog knowing he has done wrong, but that's not the case. The point of training is definitely not to make your dog afraid of you. We simply cleaned the mess up and made use of the lesson it taught us, which was that Sabre was not ready to be allowed free run of the house.

Actually, it feels good to be free of getting angry at your dog. Anger gets in the way of loving your dog, and it certainly gets in the way of thinking clearly in order to do good training. You have to learn to be tolerant of your new friend. His values are not the same as yours. He does not value the integrity of your personal possessions, so forgive his mistakes until you teach him not to be destructive. Stop blaming, and start training.

The Magic of Training the Positive Way

The magic of training with positive reinforcement and living with your dog in a positive way is the special relationship you develop with your dog. The communication is two-way, rather than the one-way communication of traditional force training. It is always exciting for me to watch a puppy who is just starting training discover this two-way communication. It can happen in a puppy as young as nine weeks. I start by using a treat to teach the puppy to sit. After a couple of repetitions, the puppy figures out that he can make you give him food by sitting in front of you. He starts to follow you around the room, sitting in front of you, without any command or signal from you. I keep rewarding the puppy with a treat. I want him to know he can get my attention by sitting, as opposed to jumping up or barking. But what I really want him to know is that he can communicate with me; I am "listening" to him.

When your training is not based on force, your dog is not inhibited from trying new behaviors out of fear of being punished. Your dog thus becomes a much more interesting companion. He shows you more of himself and his intelligence. You learn more about your dog.

Training the positive way makes you and your dog equal partners in the training. Both of you get something you want. You get the good behavior you want, and your dog gets something he wants, as when a puppy exchanges a sit for a treat. The idea of training the positive way is not to dominate a subordinate species, but to communicate with an equal but different one.

Training should be a way of making friends with your dog. (Golden Retriever)

Training should be a way of making friends with your dog. Making friends means establishing mutual understanding based on two-way communication, mutual respect, and trust. Training in a positive way will help you accomplish that goal. So let's get started!

Be prepared with treats to reward your puppy when she relieves herself outside.
(Golden Retriever)

2

Housebreaking the Positive Way

It is probably hard for you to get excited about developing a good relationship with your dog if he is defecating or urinating in your house. However, since housebreaking is the first training task most dog owners face with a new dog, it often sets the tone for their relationship. Will you start by creating distrust and fear by punishing him, or will you create trust and understanding by showing your dog in a kind way what it is you want and taking responsibility for helping him do it? Will your dog be a welcome, trusted member of the family who understands the rules, or a pain in the neck who "defies" you, in spite of being hit with a rolled up newspaper, and ruins your carpet by turning it into his bathroom?

Failure to be housebroken may mean a lifetime of being kept outside, isolated from everyone, or it may mean a dog may suffer from being punished constantly for relieving himself indoors. For all too many dogs, failure to be housebroken results in a one-way trip to the local dog pound.

If your dog is already housebroken, you don't need to read this chapter, although you still might find it interesting to glance over. It contains some good examples of using punishment versus positive reinforcement. Skip this chapter only if your dog is *really* housebroken. That means no accidents in the house unless your dog is sick or kept inside longer than he is used to. If you have a male dog, you may want to read the discussion of castration in the section on marking.

Housebreaking the positive way will rely on rewarding your dog for relieving himself where you want him to and on controlling his environment to help him form good habits. This method of housebreaking is designed to teach your dog to relieve himself only outdoors. If you live in a large city where you do not have access to a grassy area and have to teach your dog to relieve himself indoors or at a curb of the street, you should refer to a book that teaches this kind of housebreaking.

These techniques apply whether you are trying to housebreak a seven-week-old puppy or an older dog. In some ways it is more difficult to housebreak an older dog because it is hard to change an established habit of relieving himself indoors, but an older dog has the advantage of having better control than a young puppy.

We will not be doing any paper-training. It is not necessary and can be very confusing for a dog when the papers are removed.

Punishment

Talking about punishment probably seems like a funny way to start a section on housebreaking the positive way. However, punishment is the method many people use to housebreak their dogs, so I want to discuss it right away. Punishment is the cause of a lot of housebreaking problems that can be prevented. You can housebreak your dog without using it at all, which is nicer for both you and your dog and avoids getting your relationship off to a bad start.

All the disadvantages of punishment that were presented in the first chapter apply to housebreaking. The main problem is that it only tells a dog what you don't want, not what you want. Not only does punishment not tell a dog where you want him to relieve himself, but it sometimes isn't even effective at telling a dog where you *don't* want him to go. When punished for relieving themselves in the house, some dogs learn not to relieve themselves in their owner's presence, but to wait until their owners are gone or to hide and relieve themselves in another room. Once this pattern is established, it is very difficult to break.

This problem can reach incredible extremes. Puff, a three-year-old Bichon Frise, was a typical example of the dogs I see. He had never been housebroken and was brought to me when his owners were moving from their trailer with a linoleum floor to a house with new carpeting. Puff had been punished when he relieved himself in the house, so he had learned to relieve himself only when no one was around. If this meant occasionally waiting for more than 12 hours to find a chance, Puff waited that long.

One of the interesting characteristics that Puff had in common with other dogs who have been punished for accidents is that he wouldn't relieve himself outside. Puff's owners did not have a fenced yard, so they walked him on leash. Unfortunately, Puff had learned the consequences of relieving himself when his owners were present, and since being on leash meant his owners were around, he had decided not to go on leash, either. Puff's owners had kept punishing him for three years in spite of their obvious lack of success because they didn't know what else to do, and thus kept reinforcing Puff's ideas. Not only had they not managed to housebreak Puff, they had also created an aggression problem. Puff had started to defend himself from what he perceived to be unreasonable attacks by biting.

Often dogs with this misunderstanding relieve themselves in the least-used room in the house. While it may seem that they have a predilection for Oriental carpets, the real reason they are choosing the most expensive carpet in the house is that it is in a room used only for company. This problem also can be confusing if one person in the family is doing most of the punishment, or is punishing more harshly, so the dog acts differently around this person.

Do you recognize some characteristics of your dog in Puff's story? If yes, maybe your dog has received the same wrong message from your punishment. If so, then the first thing you have to do is *stop punishing*. No matter how hard it may be if you see your dog scurrying out of a room as you enter and find he has just relieved himself there, do nothing other than clean it up. To those of you who are just starting housebreaking, learn a lesson from Puff, and don't punish. It does more harm than good.

Reward

The most important thing to do when housebreaking your dog is to reward him for doing what you want, relieving himself outside. This reward can take the form of praise, but housebreaking will go faster if you use food rewards in addition to praise. It's simple to do. Every time your dog relieves himself outside, give him a treat. What you want is for your dog to rush to relieve himself when you take him outside, then run to you for his treat.

In order to reward your dog for relieving himself outside, you must *always* go outside with him, even if you have a fenced yard. Keep the treats right by the door so you can grab some as you go out. If you want to teach your dog to relieve himself in one particular place in the yard, take him to that place and stay with him until he does. You may want to keep the treats outside by this area in a plastic container. Don't let your dog play until he has relieved himself. You want to establish a habit of him relieving himself before you play, go for walks, or get into the car. You can encourage your dog to use a particular area by placing his feces or the paper towels that you have used to clean up his urine there.

If your dog has been punished and will not relieve himself outside when you are there, you will need to be more patient and do some extra things to get your dog to go outside so you can reward him and communicate what it is you want. Patience may mean staying outside with your dog and waiting for an hour until you can finally reward him. Once he understands what you want, he will get faster and faster at relieving himself.

Some dogs who have had a severe reaction to being punished absolutely refuse to relieve themselves outside on leash. Sometimes they will urinate but not defecate. Dogs have more control over their bowel movements, and often the dog has been caught more frequently in the act of defecating and has consequently been punished for that more often. One easy thing to change is to get a longer leash if the one you are using is only four or six feet in length. Your dog may feel more comfortable if he can get farther away from you. You can make a long leash (20 to 40 feet) out of a piece of rope tied to a bolt snap. This is also a good tool for teaching a dog to come when called and is further described in chapter 6. If you still cannot get your dog to defecate outside, talk to your veterinarian about using a baby suppository.

Confinement and Using a Crate

Confinement is necessary to prevent accidents when you cannot watch your dog and to encourage him to control his bladder and bowels. Most dogs will instinctively not relieve themselves when confined in a small enough area.

The most effective and safest way to confine your dog is in a crate. A crate is a small cage for dogs. Some dog owners may be upset by the idea of caging their dogs. This is understandable; it seems cruel. However, the fact of the matter is that most dogs, after they get used to their crates, *love* them. They grow attached to them. The crates provide a sense of security. If you watch your dog, you will notice that he naturally chooses places to sleep where either he is under something or his back is up against something. Most dog owners find that even after their dogs are housebroken and no longer need to be crated, they continue to sleep in their crates by choice. I often think about the fact that my dogs have a special place to go when they want to be left alone and get away from the world, but I don't!

Crates can be made of plastic, which are often the kind used for shipping dogs by air, or of metal wire. Either kind is good for housebreaking. Each has its advantages and disadvantages. The plastic crates are solid and prevent air circulation, which keeps a dog warmer, but may be too warm in hot temperatures. The metal wire crates are often collapsible, which is convenient for taking them with you if you travel with your dog. They provide good air circulation, and can be covered to keep out drafts, if necessary. Some dogs seem to like being able to see out of the metal crates, while others like being hidden in the plastic crates. Crates can be purchased at pet supply stores and through dog supply catalogs.

For a crate to work best for housebreaking, it needs to be the appropriate size. If it is too big, your dog will be able to eliminate in one end and sleep in the other. The crate should be big enough for him to lie down comfortably, stand up, and turn around, but no larger. It is okay if your dog cannot hold his head up all the way when he is standing or sitting in the crate. For example, a good size crate for a 65-pound Golden Retriever is 26 inches high,

These are two different types of crates. The dogs standing beside them show the proper size crate for that dog. (Belgian Tervuren, Greyhound)

36 inches long, and 24 inches wide. A good rule of thumb is to buy a crate that is 2 to 4 inches taller than the height of your dog at his shoulders.

Buying the right size crate to housebreak a puppy is a more difficult task. The right size crate for an eight-week-old puppy is going to be quickly outgrown. Since some dogs may need to be kept in a crate as adult dogs for reasons other than housebreaking problems, such as destructive behavior when left alone, it is more practical to purchase the size crate your dog will need as an adult. If you do this and find that your puppy is relieving himself in the crate, find a way to block off part of the crate, such as with a piece of plywood. If you think your dog will be spending a lot of time in the crate, you might want to give your dog a little more room to move around by buying one size larger than necessary.

When you get your crate, you will have to choose a place to put it. There are many options. I like keeping mine in my bedroom. In fact, I have made covers for the crates to match my bedspreads! While my dogs are young puppies and I have to use the crates frequently, I move the crates into the kitchen area during the day. The kitchen is a popular place to keep a crate, if your kitchen is large enough. Puppies are often confined to kitchens anyway because of the easy-to-clean floor, and the kitchen is a place where the family spends a lot of time. Other good places to put a crate are in a utility room, the family room, or a room of the house that isn't used often.

You may want to put some sort of bedding in the crate. Obviously, washable bedding is a good idea. Many dogs like the washable, imitation pieces of fleece that are available for dogs. If your dog shows any inclination to chew his bedding, however, you will have to remove it. Swallowing fabric can cause a life-threatening intestinal blockage. My dogs have their own personal preferences regarding bedding in their crates. Our Belgian Tervuren consistently pulls out anything we put in his crate before he goes into it. On the other hand, our Greyhound has little natural padding of her own, so she appreciates as much padding as we can stuff into her crate.

To introduce your puppy or dog to his new crate, set the crate up and allow your dog to examine it. Put treats in the crate, at first near the door, then later toward the back so he has to go all the way in to get them. Avoid forcing your dog into the crate. Throughout the first day or two, drop treats into the back of the crate every few hours. When your dog is walking in and out freely, without any fear, start feeding him in his crate. Up until now, you should not have closed the door, but once he is contentedly eating in his crate, you can close and latch the door while he is eating. Gradually extend the period of time he is shut in.

If at any time your dog starts barking, whining, or pawing at the door of the crate because he wants to be let out, *do not let him out*. Ignore his efforts to get your attention, or tell him "no" in a firm tone of voice. Don't let him out until he is quiet and has settled down. You don't want him to learn that he can get you to open the door by carrying on.

Start associating a command with putting your dog in his crate. Take your dog to his crate (dog treat in hand), throw the treat in, then give him the command as he enters the crate. My command is a highly unoriginal "get in your crate." I have a student who refers to her dog's crate as her "apartment." How long should you keep your dog in his crate? This is a difficult question to answer. A young puppy of 7 to 12 weeks of age cannot hold his urine for more than a few hours, so don't crate him longer than that, except at night. Gradually build up to four hours. By 12 weeks of age, your puppy should be able to go eight hours at night while he is sleeping. You should avoid crating your dog for more than four to five hours if at all possible, except at night.

Warning: *Never put your dog in a crate with a collar on.* He could catch his collar on part of the crate and strangle himself in his struggle to get free. Many dogs have. This is true for any kind of collar. Don't take chances.

There are other ways to confine a dog besides using a crate. One way is to keep your dog on leash and with you wherever you are in the house. You can tie the leash to a piece of furniture while you are in the room, or to your bed at night. Another way is to tie your dog with a short chain (approximately four feet long) to a screw eye fastened into your wall in a place you spend a lot of time, such as the kitchen. However, you should *never* leave your dog alone on such a chain. He could get tangled and choke himself, or he may chew on whatever furniture or baseboard is within reach.

Laundry rooms or bathrooms can work, if the rooms are small enough and aren't carpeted, and your dog won't be destructive. Cover the floor with newspaper at first. Remove anything your dog may get into, like toilet paper, soap, and towels hanging down. Your dog will probably object strenuously if you shut the door to this room while you are home. It is amazing what dog claws can do to a door. If you have to confine him there when you are home, it would be better to block the door with a baby gate. That way your puppy will feel less isolated.

Some people confine their dogs in basements, back porches, or garages while they are away. However, these places are not small enough to inhibit a dog from relieving himself. Housebreaking in the rest of the house may be more difficult because your dog may have trouble understanding that he can relieve himself in one part of the house but not in the rest.

Some dogs will relieve themselves even though they are confined to a small space. Dogs from pet shops who have been confined in small cages where they have no choice but to relieve themselves in their cages lose their normal inhibitions against this. Confinement sometimes doesn't work with them, or it takes longer to work. Also, if a dog is relieving himself inside the crate, even though he has not been left there long, it may be a sign that your dog has a bladder infection. See "Health Problems," later in this chapter for more information about this.

Other dogs panic at being confined and relieve themselves out of fear. These dogs may adjust, given time and careful handling, but some may not. I experienced this kind of problem with my Greyhound, Zephyr. Even though she was seven weeks old when I got her and introduced her to the crate, she took what seemed like forever to adjust to it. In the meantime, I cleaned up several accidents in the crate. I had never had this problem with any of my previous dogs. I think she had problems adjusting because she was a very energetic puppy and tended to be overemotional about everything. She stopped defecating in her crate in a few days, and stopped urinating in it two weeks later. In spite of her poor start, Zephyr loves her crate and now happily runs to it from anywhere in the house whenever I say, "Get in your crate." Of course, the dog biscuit she always gets when I put her in the crate probably helps a lot. If your dog does not adjust to the crate, try some of the other alternatives listed in this chapter.

Please give crate training a chance, even if you have serious misgivings. I had those same feelings when I was first introduced to the idea of a crate. I didn't believe dogs would really love them as much as they do. Many dogs who were destroyed each year because they couldn't be housebroken or were destructive when left alone could have been saved with crate training.

Confinement When You Work All Day

Housebreaking and confining your puppy or dog while you are away at work eight or more hours each day present special problems that demand special solutions. A puppy cannot go eight hours without relieving himself until he

Another means of confinement is a playpen. (Belgian Tervuren)

is five or six months old. While he is young, or while an older dog is being housebroken, you must confine him in a space large enough to permit him to sleep in a separate area from where he relieves himself, but small enough to encourage him to try to control his eliminations.

A bathroom or utility room will do, as mentioned above, but it has to be larger if your dog is going to be left there for longer hours. Put down newspapers in one part of the room, and something for your dog to lie on in another part. Leave him a small amount of water. My Borzoi was housebroken by being left in a bathroom while I was at work. It was very effective, and throughout her life, Carla loved sleeping in the bathroom, wrapped around the cool base of the toilet or curled up in the bathtub. In fact, we had to tie the bathroom door open when we were gone because oftentimes Carla would stretch out on the cool tile floor and shut the door on herself by mistake.

Another option is to use an exercise pen set up inside. This is a pen without a top or bottom, and it usually folds flat for storage. They are made of eight connecting wire panels, ranging in height from 24 inches to 45 inches. There are also plastic pens called play yards. These are used for both puppies and babies, so you can also find these where baby supplies are sold. They are very lightweight. You can put a sheet of plastic underneath, and then cover the area with newspapers.

If you confine your dog in the kitchen, I would suggest blocking off part of the room. Most kitchens are too big for effective housebreaking. With a little ingenuity, you can build a barrier, perhaps with a hinged gate to allow easy access.

You can still use a crate to housebreak your dog, but arrangements need to be made to let your dog out halfway through the day. If you cannot arrange to come home from work over your lunch hour during the few weeks or months it may take to housebreak your dog, perhaps you can persuade a neighbor, relative, or friend to drop by and let your dog out. Offer an exchange for their help. Perhaps you could take care of their pet when they are away on a weekend. You could also hire someone to come in and let your dog out to relieve himself.

Some people leave their dogs outdoors in a kennel or fenced yard while they are away at work. Unfortunately, this is often not safe for your dog. First of all, dogs are stolen out of such enclosures. If you are using a fenced yard, your dog could learn to climb the fence while you are gone. Your dog is help-lessly exposed to the teasing of neighborhood children, and this can lead to an aggression problem. Your dog may develop a barking problem that annoys your neighbors. The safest place to leave your dog is inside your house.

When you are home, continue to restrict your dog's freedom and super-vise him closely to prevent accidents. Pick up any soiled newspapers as soon as you get home, and do not put down fresh ones until you are ready to leave the next morning. The papers are only being used to protect your floor, not to paper-train your dog. Don't let your dog use them when you are home. If your dog tries to relieve himself where he is kept during the day while you are at home, block off that room or area.

Giving Your Dog More Freedom

One of the most common mistakes people make when housebreaking their dogs is giving them too much freedom too soon. If your 7- to 12-week-old puppy is having more than one accident every three days, you are giving him too much freedom. The same holds true for a three- to five-month-old puppy who is having more than one accident a week, and for a dog over five months old who is having any accidents.

A good time to give your dog more freedom is right after you have taken him out and seen him relieve himself. If he is in the 7- to 12-week age range, limit this to 15 minutes to half an hour, and keep him in one room. When he looks like he is about to take a nap, put him back in his crate and shut the door. Gradually give him more time out of the crate and access to more rooms, one room at a time. The use of expandable baby gates is invaluable. They come extra-tall and extra-wide, and can even be double-stacked if your dog is a good climber or jumper. If your dog has an accident, you've given him too much freedom and need to cut back.

There can be a problem with confining your dog too much. For example, a puppy kept exclusively in a kitchen until he is six months old may not regard the rest of the house as part of his home that he instinctively wants to keep clean. While your puppy is young, or while you are in the process of house-breaking an adult dog, it is wise to give him brief, supervised access to whatever rooms in the house the dog will be allowed in when he is housebroken.

You will also want to try giving your dog more freedom when you are away from home. Again, start with one room. Try it when you are going out for a short errand. Slowly extend the time you leave your dog alone, and add more rooms.

Do not assume that because your dog is housebroken in your house, he will not eliminate in other people's homes. Even if he is perfect at home, restrict his freedom in other people's homes by keeping him on leash until you are sure you can trust him. It is best to avoid mortifying experiences, like the time our young male dog lifted his leg on my sister-in-law's Christmas tree!

Scheduling

It is easiest to housebreak your dog if you keep him on a schedule. He will know when to expect to be taken out to relieve himself, and you will learn when he needs to go.

Start by feeding your dog on a schedule. Pick convenient times, with the number of meals dependent on the age of your puppy, and stick with these times, even on weekends. Do not leave food available during the day. If your dog doesn't finish what you put down, pick it up and either save it or throw it away.

If you feed your dog at the same times every day, he should have to defecate at corresponding times. You'll be able to predict when these times are. To learn what your dog's schedule is, keep a housebreaking diary. Write down for five days what time you feed your dog, how much he eats (more about amounts of food later), when he defecates, when he urinates, where he eliminates (in the house or outside!), and what he was doing right before he urinated. You will need to get all the members of your family to cooperate.

Soon you should begin to see a pattern. Your dog should defecate at approximately the same times each day. If these times are not convenient for you, gradually change his feeding times. When your dog urinates is probably more related to what he is doing than what time it is. Dogs usually have to urinate when they first wake up in the morning and when they wake up from any naps during the day. Puppies are especially susceptible to lack of bladder control when they get excited and are playing.

Your housebreaking diary will identify the times when your puppy or dog has accidents in the house. Use this information to figure out what you are doing wrong and what you can do to solve it. Perhaps at certain times of the day you are too busy, and your dog is not being supervised adequately. Is it when the kids get home from school, or when you are fixing dinner? Whenever these times occur, you may want to confine your dog. Are the

A sample housebreaking diary.

accidents occurring in one place in the house? Maybe you are not completely getting the smell of the urine or stool out of the carpet, and so the smell is attracting your dog back to the same place. Is your dog only having accidents in rooms when you aren't there? Your dog may be confused by your punishment.

Feeding

As discussed above, feeding your dog on a schedule will make housebreaking easier. How much and what you feed your dog will also have an effect.

It helps if you feed your dog a high-quality dry dog food. The better-quality dog foods have less filler in them, thereby producing a smaller volume of feces, less frequent bowel movements, and firm stools. Dry dog food is best because it is more economical than canned dog food, is better for your dog's teeth, and does not contain the chemicals and sugars of the semimoist, burger-type dog foods. Many people are not aware that most of the premium-quality dry dog foods are not sold in supermarkets. These foods cost more but usually are fed in smaller quantities. They are available in pet stores and at some kennels. If you are having a housebreaking problem with defecating in the house, it is worth trying one of these foods.

Like people, all dogs react differently to different foods. What agrees with your neighbor's dog may cause diarrhea in yours. Also, if you keep switching foods, your dog's intestines will have to keep readjusting, and he may have intermittent diarrhea from this. Once you have found a dog food that is good for your dog, stick to it. Feed the same amount of the same food every day, keeping in mind your dog's changing nutritional needs as he matures. Don't add table scraps, and don't give between-meal treats except as necessary for training. These rules may be relaxed when your dog is completely housebroken, but not until then. It is hard enough for your dog to control his bowels when you are gone for long periods of time. Don't make it harder on him by feeding him improperly.

Another feeding problem that interferes with housebreaking is feeding your dog too much. It is hard to tell what amount to feed a dog, especially a growing puppy. This is complicated by the fact that the amounts suggested on the bag of dog food are too much for most dogs. Overfeeding can cause frequent bowel movements and stools of soft consistency, which makes it harder for your dog to control his bowels. It can even cause diarrhea. One way to tell if you are overfeeding your dog is by noting the consistency of his stools, which should be firm. If your dog is not finishing the food you give him, he is probably being overfed. While fat, roly-poly puppies may be appealing, it is

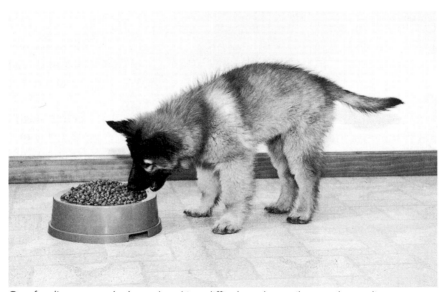

Overfeeding can make housebreaking difficult and contribute to bone diseases. (Belgian Tervuren)

better for your dog's health to keep him on the slim side. Overfeeding has been shown to exacerbate some diseases, such as hip dysplasia.

Cleaning Up

It is important that any accidents your dog has in your house be thoroughly cleaned up. If there is any remaining scent, the smell will attract your dog to relieve himself in that area again.

The thing *not* to use to clean up urine or feces is an ammonia-based product. Urine contains ammonia, so you are just adding more if you use such a product. The lingering ammonia smell may attract your dog back to the place you just cleaned up.

The best cleaning products are those specially designed for this purpose. They are available in pet stores or sometimes at veterinarians. Bacteria/enzyme products work best. Look for this on the label. If you are doing a good job with housebreaking and accidents are kept to a minimum, it may not be necessary to purchase such a product. Instead you can use a mixture of half water and half white distilled vinegar. This is convenient to use if kept in a spray bottle.

Whatever you use, blot up the urine well. Do it as soon as possible to prevent the urine from spreading deeper into the carpet. Remove as much moisture as possible. Then follow the directions on the pet stain cleaning product or spray with the vinegar-water mixture. Blot some more, then place a thick stack of paper towels on the spot and weigh it down with a heavy book. Put aluminum foil or plastic wrap between the book and towels to protect the book.

Asking to Go Out

Many dog owners are concerned because their dogs don't ask to go out. Many dogs do not, and this is not necessary to housebreak a dog. You should be taking your dog out on a regular enough basis and frequently enough that he doesn't have to ask to go out.

Some dogs learn to ask to go out on their own, without being taught. These are usually dogs with more assertive personalities. A passive dog may never ask to go out, or he may give hard-to-read signs, such as pacing, whining, or just looking uncomfortable.

I've had some dogs who ask to go out, and some who did not. Zephyr, my Greyhound, asked to go out by standing at the back door, hitting the doorknob with her nose, and whining. She learned to do this on her own. Sabre, our first Belgian Tervuren, never asked to go out. Interestingly, if Sabre was sick and needed to go out right away, he communicated this to us by staring at us. If he was desperate, he would wake us up at night or stand by the back door. Even though Sabre knew how to ask to go out, he did not do so except in emergencies. And Sabre *never* had an accident in the house from the time he was a puppy.

There are, in fact, disadvantages to having a dog learn to ask to go out. Some dogs will start asking to go out whenever they want their owner's attention, or just to play outside. It is hard to tell if the dog has to relieve himself or not.

If you think it would be helpful in your situation, you can teach your dog to ask to go out. Before you take him out the door, take his paw and hit it against the door. Another option is to tie bells to the doorknob for your dog to ring. Hang the bells so they are on the dog's level. You can also use a set of the sleigh bells people hang on their doorknobs during the Christmas season. Hit the bells with your dog's paw before you go out. Once your dog is housebroken, you can take the bells down if your dog is ringing them constantly for attention.

This dog is hitting bells to indicate he wants to go out. (Shetland Sheepdog)

Realistic Expectations

I want to give you some idea of what you can realistically expect when housebreaking your dog. How fast this program can work depends on many factors. An excitable puppy will take longer than a laid-back one. Housebreaking in a busy household in which chaos rules is harder than in a quiet one on a regular schedule. And an older dog with a well-established habit of relieving himself inside will take longer than a puppy or an older dog who has been previously kept outside.

If you start with a 7- to 12-week-old puppy and follow the above program religiously, you may be able to limit the number of accidents in your house to three or four times per week. However, if your puppy is under four months old, it is to be expected that he will sometimes lose control of his bladder when he gets excited. If you are following this program and after three weeks are having more than a few accidents a week, you are probably doing something wrong. Check the troubleshooting list at the end of this chapter, and reread the chapter.

Your dog should be completely housebroken by the time he is six months old. By *completely housebroken* I mean able to be taken with complete confidence to visit your mother-in-law who is not very fond of dogs and has expensive Oriental carpets.

If you feel your dog is not progressing fast enough in his housebreaking, seek the help of a professional dog trainer who counsels clients about this problem. The longer your dog continues to relieve himself in the house, the harder it will be to housebreak him. Don't wait too long!

Submissive Urination

Some dogs lose control of their bladders when they greet people, either family members or strangers. This is different from other housebreaking problems. It is called *submissive urination* by dog behaviorists. It is a normal canine greeting behavior. A dog who does this has no conscious control over his urination at the time. This is a common behavior in puppies, and usually goes away as they mature. Some dogs are as old as two years before they stop submissively urinating. Rarely it may persist in some dogs throughout their lives. Submissive urination can be a difficult problem to solve, but there are some things you can do to help.

First of all, because your dog has no conscious control over it, punishment will certainly not help. In fact, it will make things worse because the punishment will increase his submissive behavior. Even a slightly raised voice to a dog with this problem will cause him to urinate submissively. The best thing to do when this happens is to simply ignore it and clean it up.

If your dog urinates in excitement when you arrive home, make your arrival as calm and matter-of-fact as possible. When you get home, try not to talk to him for the first five minutes. Of course, try to greet your dog outside to eliminate cleanup. You might also try distracting your dog with a treat or by throwing a ball if he is a compulsive retriever.

The best thing you can do for this problem is to build your dog's confidence. Take him to different places and let him meet as many people as possible. Attending an obedience training class is a great way to do this. Your dog will get exposure to a different place and to people and other dogs. Bring a roll of paper towels to the first few classes in case of accidents.

Marking

If you have a male dog who is lifting his leg on your furniture, your housebreaking problem may be hormonally related. The best solution is castration, which removes the source of the hormones that cause this housebreaking problem. The sex-related hormones that are released in a male dog as he sexually matures cause your dog to have urges to mark his territory by urinating on upright objects. While castration is not a 100 percent cure, it works well most of the time, combined with other housebreaking techniques. This does not mean it is impossible to housebreak an intact male. However, if you have this problem, housebreaking will be much easier if your dog is castrated.

The strength of the urge to mark varies in male dogs. In some, the urge seems to be so strong that it is almost beyond their conscious control. These dogs are often described by their owners as "high-strung" or "hyper." They are sometimes hard to keep weight on. Castration helps all these problems. Some dogs become housebroken within days after surgery, after many months of marking problems.

Castration is an emotionally charged subject for many dog owners. It is perfectly understandable that people feel uncomfortable about surgically removing part of their dog's anatomy. Many people are afraid of how their dog might change. Still others are attracted to the idea of using their dog at stud. However, dogs only change for the better following castration. Dogs who protect the house continue to do so; hunting dogs work just as well after as before. Some dogs gain weight following castration. They simply need to have the amount of food they eat reduced. If the weight gain doesn't respond to a change in diet, you might want to have your veterinarian run a thyroid test on your dog, which requires analysis of a blood sample.

People often want to have their male dog sire a litter of puppies because they love their male dogs and want to see their good qualities reproduced. Making money and satisfying a male dog's sexual urges are other reasons people want to use their dogs at stud, even though these are poor reasons. Unfortunately, there are millions of unwanted dogs killed every year. The world doesn't need more dogs. Only the very best male dogs should be used at stud — those who have been screened by experts for the genetic problems that plague dogs, have had their pedigrees examined by someone knowledgeable, and have been judged by someone both knowledgeable and objective (not the owner or breeder of the dog) to be outstanding specimens of their breed. Realistically, the chances are slim that an owner of a quality female dog will want to use your dog at stud.

It is kinder to castrate your dog than to subject him to a lifetime of being punished, even if it's just verbally, for urinating in the house. Uncastrated male dogs are not genetically cut out to live in the world they find themselves in as our pets and are often cruelly frustrated. Castration is a simple, safe surgical procedure that will reduce your dog's cancer risks and the chance of prostate problems, as well as make his life more comfortable emotionally.

Health Problems

If you are having problems housebreaking your dog, it is imperative that you make sure he does not have a health problem. The most common is a bladder infection. Male or female dogs can have this problem, and the symptoms are easy to overlook. Bladder infections are more common in young puppies, whose immune systems are not mature enough to combat infections. And don't be fooled by the fact that your puppy has had a veterinary examination when he got his shots. The veterinarian cannot tell if your puppy has a bladder infection by an examination. The only way to check is with a urine sample. You can collect this sample at home and take it in while it is still fresh, or refrigerate it until you can get it to the veterinarian. Of course, collecting the sample may provide any nosy neighbors with a lot of entertainment.

One of the symptoms of a bladder infection is frequent urination of small amounts. A dog with a bladder infection will often relieve himself in his crate. If you suspect your puppy is relieving himself more often than normal, you would be wise to have a urine sample checked. Bladder infections are treated with antibiotics.

There are other causes for lack of bladder control, such as an obstructed bladder, an enlarged prostate gland, or kidney failure. Older female dogs who have been spayed sometimes start to lose control over their bladder because they have a deficiency of estrogen, a hormone that is important in maintaining the bladder tone. This can be treated by a veterinarian. Frequent urination and lack of bladder control can be a side effect of cortisone, a drug used often in veterinary medicine.

I'll never forget the story of Buttons, a cute, shaggy three-year-old mixed breed who signed up for one of my obedience classes. Buttons just didn't seem healthy. There was something about the look in her eyes, and she lacked the stamina to work for the whole hour of the class. I expressed my concern to her owner and asked about Buttons' health, including if she was having frequent urination or housebreaking problems. She said no, although questioning did reveal that Buttons had been on cortisone for flea-allergy

Catching a urine sample can be awkward but necessary if you suspect a bladder infection. (German Shorthaired Pointer)

problems for many months. Repeated questioning over the next few weeks finally elicited the information that Buttons was paper-trained because she could not hold her urine for very long. Her owner had never had another dog and assumed that this was normal! I quickly sent her off to her veterinarian and, sure enough, Buttons had a bladder infection. Who knows how long she had had it, since the veterinarian had noted a slightly elevated temperature on her last exam a year previous! It could have been that the immunosuppressive nature of the cortisone made Buttons at increased risk for getting a bladder infection. In any case, after 10 days of treatment with antibiotics and elimination of the cortisone, Buttons' owner picked up the newspapers and never had to use them again. In addition, her "couch potato" dog was full of new energy, able to play and participate in the family activities.

Another health problem that interferes with housebreaking is diarrhea. There are many causes of diarrhea, some of which can be frustrating to diagnose

Buttons. (Mixed breed)

and cure. The effect of overfeeding on stool volume and consistency has already been discussed. Among the causes of diarrhea are worms, protozoan infections, food intolerance, pancreatic enzyme deficiency, and viruses. You and your veterinarian must be persistent in searching for the right cause and the right treatment.

Troubleshooting Checklist

Still having trouble with accidents in the house? Maybe you've missed something in this chapter. Go over this checklist carefully, and see if there is something you are not doing.

1. Are you keeping your dog confined when you cannot watch him, even if you are in the house with him?
2. Did you keep a housebreaking diary for five days?
3. Are you careful to feed your dog at the same time every day? Measuring his food? Not overfeeding? No snacks? No table scraps? Not switching foods?

4. Is everyone in your family cooperating in your housebreaking efforts?

5. Are you punishing your dog and confusing him?

6. Are you sure your dog isn't sick and needs to be checked by a veterinarian?

7. Do you always go outside with your dog so that you know whether he has relieved himself and so you are able to reward him?

8. Are you completely getting the scent of your dog's urine and/or stools out of the carpet?

9. Are you giving your dog too much freedom in the house?

10. Are you expecting too much self-control from a young puppy?

Housebreaking works best when combined with obedience training that helps you and your dog understand each other better, so let's move on.

3

Getting Off to a Good Start

It is much easier to train a dog, and your chances of success are much greater, if you get off to a good start. Ideally, this means starting when you bring your puppy home, at between 7 and 12 weeks of age. If you have a puppy between those ages, this chapter is for you.

Many of you reading this book probably already have a dog older than 12 weeks. Unfortunately, some people don't seek training information until after they have gotten off to a *bad* start and are having trouble with their dog. Even if your dog is older than 12 weeks, you should read this chapter. You can compare the positive training method with how your dog was handled in his first 12 weeks, or if you don't know, how you guess he was handled, and that will help you understand your dog now. You'll be more patient when training your older dog if you understand that he lacked the advantages of being trained at an early age.

Whether you are starting with a puppy or with an older dog you've just adopted, or are trying to build a new relationship with a dog you've had for a while, you will begin by teaching commands in the way described under "Teaching Commands: Sit, Stay, Okay, and No." No matter what your dog's age, he needs to have his confidence built up through socialization; this process is discussed in "Building Confidence." The first section is about choosing a dog. Discovering the mistakes you made in choosing your dog may help prevent you from blaming him for not being what you expected. You will be better prepared next time you get a dog. You could even pass this information along to a friend who is getting a dog!

Choosing a Dog

Getting off to a good start begins with choosing the right dog. Remember the discussion about realistic expectations in the first chapter? I said it was possible to have your own super dog if you use the right care, the right training, and the right dog. Getting the right dog is an important part of this equation. Part of the television myth that leads people to have unrealistic expectations is the belief that dogs are basically all alike and, with enough love, any dog can become a great pet. Unfortunately, this just isn't true. Some dogs are born with bad temperaments that no amount of love and training can fix, or health problems that will run up expensive veterinary bills.

Selecting a good dog is a process full of pitfalls. However, you can maximize your chances of getting the perfect dog for you by making well-informed choices. If you already have a dog, compare this information with how you chose him. It may help you understand your dog better.

Among your first choices are purebred versus mixed breed, puppy versus older dog, and whether to rescue a dog from a Humane Society shelter or go to a breeder. Another option is to adopt a purebred dog from one of the non-profit rescue groups that specialize in one breed. These decisions depend partially on your personal preferences, but try to be aware of the problems you can run into. Dogs do have hereditary health and temperament problems, whether purebred or mixed. Because the gene pool is limited in purebred dogs in order to maintain breed type, some health problems can become more frequent. Some examples are epilepsy in Irish Setters and hip dysplasia in Labrador Retrievers and Rottweilers. The good news is that good breeders are aware of these diseases and test for them. Then, they carefully breed to eliminate them. The breeders who do this most likely also show their dogs. Don't avoid show dog breeders, even though you just want a pet. People who go to the trouble of showing their dogs and care enough to get a judge's opinion about the quality of their dogs are careful breeders. Most breedings of show dogs produce some pet quality puppies. These pet quality puppies benefit from the same health screenings, temperament considerations, and enriched environments. Show dogs have to tolerate the stress of being around hundreds of strange dogs, having their teeth and testicles checked, and looking happy about it. Wouldn't you like a dog able to handle that kind of stress?

The worst place to buy a dog is from a pet shop. They sell poor quality dogs at ridiculously high prices. The conditions in which these dogs are bred are cruel. I live near puppy mills. One had 431 dogs plus several puppies. These dogs live in filthy wire cages and never see daylight. Obviously, this "breeder" isn't screening for health and temperament problems. Some people buy puppies at pet shops because they think rescuing them is good. In reality, people are making financial donations to animal cruelty.

It is easy to be deceived about the quality of a purebred dog. This deception is often unintentional on the part of the breeders, who may themselves be uninformed about the quality of the dogs they are breeding. Buyers of purebred dogs often wrongly interpret statements such as these:

"These dogs are AKC registered." AKC registration has nothing to do with the quality of a dog. The American Kennel Club does not screen dogs for good temperament or absence of hereditary health problems before they register them. The only thing AKC registration means is that the puppy was the result of a mating of two registered dogs. Even that isn't guaranteed, as it is possible to obtain registration papers under false pretenses.

"These dogs are from champion lines." Puppy buyers are often impressed by seeing a champion or two on a pedigree, even though these champions are several generations removed from the puppy they are considering purchasing. Unfortunately, any influence these champions may have had on the quality of a dog can be negated by one indiscriminate breeding. If these champions are not your puppy's sire or dam, don't be mistakenly impressed by them. An AKC championship is not an absolute guarantee of quality anyway. It is possible to show a dog with hip dysplasia, a hereditary disease that affects a dog's hip joint, to a championship.

"My dogs have never had any trouble with hip dysplasia." Some puppy buyers have done enough research on the breed they are purchasing to know that the breed has hereditary problems, such as hip dysplasia. When they ask about it, the above statement may be the answer they receive. The only way hip dysplasia can be reliably diagnosed is with an X ray of the sire and dam prior to breeding. These X rays are then often submitted to the Orthopedic Foundation for Animals (OFA) to be evaluated by veterinary radiologists. If the X ray shows good hip joints, the dog is then given an OFA number. This number is not given to dogs under two years of age because not all cases can be detected until then. If you hear the above line, ask if the dogs have been X-rayed.

"This is a new breed." In order to cash in on people's desire to have something unique, people often advertise a "new breed." An example from our area is a Labrador/Poodle mix. If you want to buy a mixed-breed dog, that's fine. You should know, however, that the producers of these dogs do not usually (never, in my experience) screen for health problems. Additional breeds are admitted to the AKC, but they are breeds that have existed for many years and whose breeders have become nationally organized for the several years necessary for admittance to the AKC.

"This dog is from a kennel (or breeder), not a pet shop." Some people know enough to avoid the high-priced and often low-quality puppies available at pet shops, but are unable to distinguish between good and bad breeders and kennels. Anyone who owns a female dog and breeds it is a breeder, but not necessarily a good one! Even more confusing is the term "kennel." It can refer to a breeder of show dogs who keeps her two dogs in the house and raises one litter every two years in her family room. It can also refer to someone who mass-produces puppies of several breeds without regard to quality using dogs who spend their entire lives in cages.

"This puppy comes with a guarantee." Read the fine print. Many guarantees require that you return the original puppy before you will be given a replacement. However, you will already be in love with your first puppy and unwilling to give him up, especially to an uncertain fate. And would you want another puppy from a breeder who has already been proven to produce problem dogs? Your best guarantee is careful shopping before you buy a dog.

These are just some examples of ways to be misled when purchasing a dog. Let them serve as warnings: Be careful!

Where should you look for a good puppy? The best litters are rarely advertised in newspapers. Your local kennel club may be able to refer you to a good breeder, but the club may not be listed in the phone book. A veterinarian, groomer, or boarding kennel may be able to put you in touch with the local dog club. The American Kennel Club has good breeder referral information on its Web site at akc.org. If you are getting an older dog, beware of hidden problems. People often give up an older dog because of a behavior problem, one they may not be honest about in order to place the dog in a new home. If possible, you may want to arrange for at least a one-week and preferably a one-month trial period, during which time you can return the dog if you run into a problem.

Howell Book House has published two excellent books for help in adopting older dogs. One is called *SuccessfulDog Adoption* (2003) by Sue Sternberg. This book details how to test a dog when choosing a dog from a shelter to make sure you get the right dog for you. If you are considering adopting a purebred from a breed rescue group, read *Purebred Rescue Dog Adoption: Rewards and Realities* (2004) by Liz Palika. I highly recommend them!

Good breeders keep their puppies until they are at least seven weeks old. (Belgian Tervuren)

Characteristics of a Good Breeder

Some things to look for in locating a conscientious dog breeder:

1. A good breeder only breeds one or two breeds, as it is difficult to be truly knowledgeable about more breeds than that.

2. A good breeder will not be anxious to sell you a dog until he questions you closely to see if you will be a good dog owner.

3. A good breeder will raise his puppies so that they have a lot of contact with people. The puppies will be in a clean environment.

4. A good breeder will be able to tell you the genetic problems within his particular breed and what he has done to reduce the chances of these problems occurring in the dogs he is producing.

5. A good breeder will be knowledgeable about the breed standard set by the breed's national organization and how well his dogs meet this standard.

6. A good breeder can tell you why the breeding partners were selected and what characteristics they will hopefully produce. He will also be knowledgeable about genetics and be able to tell you if the puppies are line bred or an outcross.

7. A good breeder does not sell puppies to a pet shop or another third party because he wants to have control over the homes the puppies are placed in.

8. A good breeder sells pet-quality puppies with spay-neuter agreements.

9. A good breeder breeds infrequently, usually no more than two litters a year, and often as infrequently as one litter every two years.

10. A good breeder provides complete instructions on feeding, veterinary care, etc., with each puppy, as well as a written guarantee and contract. He is anxious to educate the buyers of his puppies.

11. Good breeders are committed to the welfare of the breed as well as their individual dogs.

12. A good breeder will want to be informed if at any time you can no longer keep your dog.

13. A good breeder will show his dogs, as this is the best way of obtaining an objective opinion regarding how well a dog measures up to the breed standard.

Once you have decided on a breeder and a litter, you will be faced with the task of selecting a puppy from the litter. The best age to get a dog is between 7 and 12 weeks of age, with closer to 7 weeks being preferable. At 7 weeks of age, puppies have been with their littermates long enough to have had the experiences necessary for them to develop normally, yet they are young enough to form a fine firm bond with human beings. If puppies are removed from their litters too early or too late, behavior problems can develop.

An example of this is Macduff, a Scottish Terrier purchased from a mass-production kennel business. He was five months old when he was purchased by his owner, Joann. Joann called me because Macduff wouldn't come to her—ever. He never approached her when they were in the house. He actively avoided all her attempts to get him inside when she let Macduff out in her fenced backyard. Joann, a single woman, had recently lost an old dog and was bitterly disappointed by the lack of affection and responsiveness in her new Scottie. Macduff's behavior was the result of having been kept in a kennel isolated from people for too long. He was past the age when a puppy can best form a strong bond to humans. Fortunately, training the positive way helped him develop a relationship with his new owner, but it is unlikely that their relationship will fulfill all the potential it would have had if he had left the kennel at an earlier age.

Many personality traits that a dog will have when mature can be observed in a young puppy. Puppy behavior testing is a way of systematically making these observations. Seven weeks of age is a good time for this testing because puppies at this age are physically mature enough to be able to move around easily, but young enough to make environmental influences on the puppy's behavior minimal. The testing should be done by someone who is a stranger to the puppies. Each puppy is tested individually because puppies

This seven-week-old puppy is demonstrating his attraction to people on the social attraction part of puppy temperament testing. (Labrador Retriever)

behave differently when separated from their littermates. The testing should also be done in a place that is strange to the puppies, to test their reactions to a new location.

Although someone experienced with puppy temperament testing would do the best job of testing, especially interpreting the puppies' behavior, you can do the testing yourself. Several tests are provided here, as well as information on how to administer and interpret them. Make photocopies of the tests, with one copy for each puppy, and circle the responses. Puppies may have responses that are not listed on the test. Try to interpret these as best you can.

If you already have a dog, think about how your dog might have reacted to these tests as a puppy, and what that tells you about him now.

Puppy Temperament Tests

Social Attraction

Have someone place the puppy on the floor approximately four feet from the tester, who is kneeling on the floor. The tester coaxes the puppy to him with his voice and body motions.

Responses:
A. Puppy runs to tester with tail up, jumps up.
B. Puppy takes a few seconds to look around, then comes to tester, tail up.
C. Puppy comes hesitantly, tail down.
D. Puppy will not come at all; remains frozen in place.
E. Puppy wanders off to explore room, ignoring tester.

Meanings:
A. This puppy is bold and confident. He likes people. Will you mind a problem with your dog jumping up on people? Don't be taken in by this attractive response. Bold dogs are difficult to control.
B. Moderate response.
C. Puppy is less sure of himself, especially in a strange place, but still attracted to people. May be easier to control. See if pup's confidence increases as test progresses.
D. Puppy is scared, intolerant of stress. Look for trembling to indicate degree of fear. This puppy may be shy of strangers.
E. There may be two reasons for this response. One is that the puppy is not a people-oriented dog, preferring to satisfy his own curiosity than to seek company. His independence may make him hard to train. The other reason for this response could be that the puppy is not attracted to strangers, but may still bond well to one person.

Following

The tester stands up and walks away from the puppy, talking to the puppy encouragingly. Walk about 10 to 20 feet, if there is room.

Responses:

A. Follows readily, tail up, gets underfoot or runs ahead.
B. Follows readily, tail up.
C. Follows hesitantly, tail down.
D. Does not follow; remains frozen in place.
E. Wanders off to explore.

Meanings:

A. While attracted to people, this puppy is also assertive. May need an equally assertive owner.
B. Confident, but ready to follow owner, literally and figuratively.
C. Puppy less confident.
D. Puppy scared.
E. This puppy is independent and will be difficult to establish control of off leash.

Restraint

The tester gently places the puppy on his back and holds him there for 30 seconds.

Responses:

A. Puppy struggles fiercely, bites.
B. Puppy struggles fiercely, may bark.
C. Puppy struggles a little.
D. Puppy does not struggle, relaxed.
E. Puppy does not struggle, tense.

Meanings:

A. Avoid this puppy if you have small children. Many children are bitten when they are restraining their dog by hugging him. This dog may be hard to restrain at the veterinarian. Early and firm training will be necessary.
B. Indicates active, assertive dog, lacking in tolerance.
C. Moderate response.
D. This more passive, easygoing pup will be easier to handle.
E. Puppy scared, stressed.

The restraint test. (Labrador Retriever)

Reaction to Petting

The tester sits the puppy beside him and pets the puppy, talks to him.

Responses:
A. Puppy climbs or attempts to climb up on tester's lap; jumps at face and licks.
B. Puppy cuddles up to tester.
C. Puppy sits quietly, accepting petting.
D. Puppy crouches down, trembles.
E. Puppy goes around tester, sniffing shoes, or goes away.

Meanings:
A. The puppy loves people, but are his constant attempts to climb into your lap (and maybe everyone else's) or otherwise get your attention going to bother you? Will you enjoy it?
B. An affectionate puppy.
C. This passive puppy is either a little frightened or aloof with strangers.
D. Puppy is scared.
E. Puppy is not attracted to people and independent.

Retrieving

The tester crumples up a piece of paper and tosses it two to four feet in front of the puppy while he is looking. If he picks it up, encourage him to come back.

Responses:

A. Chases paper, grabs it, and runs off.
B. Chases paper, sniffs it, runs off.
C. Chases paper, picks it up, and returns to tester.
D. Approaches paper hesitantly, stretches nose to cautiously sniff paper.
E. Chases paper a short distance, but returns to tester.
F. Not interested; wanders off.
G. Refuses to leave tester.

Meanings:

A. Puppy may always chase things he sees, like dogs on the other side of the road. He is also exhibiting independence.
B. Same as above, with less retrieving instinct.
C. Good response; retrieving correlated with high trainability.
D. Puppy lacks confidence, but may retrieve with practice and encouragement; may also indicate pointing ability in bird-hunting dog.
E. Indicates high level of social attraction and less retrieving instinct.
F. No retrieving instinct, puppy will probably not play retrieving games; indicates independence and reduced trainability.
G. Puppy scared.

This puppy's response to the retrieving test indicates he will have a high level of trainability. (Labrador Retriever)

Touch Sensitivity

The tester cradles the puppy in lap, takes webbing between front toes between thumb and forefinger, and gradually increases pressure while counting to 10, stopping as soon as the puppy pulls his paw away.

Meaning:

Some dogs are more pain sensitive than others. Dogs who are not pain sensitive may be hard to train by traditional methods that rely on dog's discomfort. A common problem with such dogs is pulling on the leash. Other dogs may be pain sensitive and overreact to every touch, perhaps nipping when a hair gets pulled while being brushed. A middle response is desirable. Most dogs are relatively pain insensitive.

Sound Sensitivity

The tester hits the bottom of a metal pan with a metal spoon while the puppy is a few feet away. Set the pan on the ground after hitting it.

Responses:
  A. Puppy locates sound and trots to pan to investigate.
  B. Puppy looks toward direction of sound but doesn't walk toward pan.
  C. Puppy cringes, runs away, and tries to hide.

Meanings:
  A. Puppy is bold and confident, not sound shy.
  B. Puppy is less bold, but not sound shy.
  C. This amount of fear indicates sound shyness. A sound shy dog can panic during a thunderstorm, or run away when a car backfires. This would be a big problem for a hunter.

Sight Sensitivity

The tester opens an umbrella held close to the ground about four feet away from the puppy and sets the umbrella on the ground.

Responses:
  A. Puppy may or may not jump back, but then approaches umbrella on own; may mouth umbrella.
  B. Puppy may or may not jump back; approaches umbrella with encouragement.
  C. Puppy cringes, goes away, and tries to hide.

It is normal for a puppy to be startled when an umbrella is opened in the sight sensitivity test. (Labrador Retriever)

Meanings:
A.   Puppy very bold and curious, not afraid of things.
B.   Puppy less bold but not afraid.
C.   Puppy afraid of strange-looking objects; often grows up to be a dog easily "spooked."

Energy Level

Tester observes puppy during testing.

Responses:
A.   Mostly runs about, never stops.
B.   Mostly trots, mildly curious.
C.   Walks quietly about, remains in position tester puts him in.
D.   Moves very little, tense.

Meanings:
A.   High energy level. Will be hard to keep quiet and will need a *lot* of exercise.
B.   Medium energy level. Will still need exercise.
C.   Low energy level. Easy to live with.
D.   Puppy scared, stressed.

Puppy Temperament Testing

Test	Good	Fair	Undesirable
Social Attraction			
Call puppy to you	runs to you, tail up	comes hesitantly	goes away or is frightened
Following			
Puppy follows you as you walk away	follows at your heels	follows hesitantly	does not follow or bites at you
Restraint			
Puppy is held on back for 30 seconds	lies quietly, makes eye contact	struggles but settles when gently shaken	struggles fiercely, tries to bite
Reaction to Petting			
Puppy is sitting beside you on the floor, being petted	cuddles up to you, sits quietly in lap	climbs up on you, jumps at your face	goes away or is frightened
Retrieving			
Throw ball of paper about 4 feet	runs to paper, picks up and returns	chases paper but drops, returns to you	no interest or picks up and runs away
Touch Sensitivity			
Apply increasing pressure to toe webbing while counting 1–10	count of 4–7	count of 3–8	counts of 1–2 or 9–10
Sound Sensitivity			
Hit pan with metal spoon 4 feet from puppy	startles but goes to investigate pan	runs away but comes back with encouragement	runs away and hides, will not return
Sight Sensitivity			
Open umbrella 4 feet from puppy	startles but approaches umbrella to investigate	runs away but approaches umbrella with encouragement	runs away and hides, will not return
Energy Level			
	medium: trots around exploring surroundings	quiet: doesn't move around much	runs constantly

This 10-week-old Basset Hound puppy is learning to sit with food.

Starting Training

Training starts the minute you bring your puppy home. Communication begins immediately, whether it is part of a carefully planned training program or not. Your puppy is learning from all his interactions with you, and by planning your training from the start, you can make sure you and your puppy develop the relationship you want to have. Between the ages of 7 and 12 weeks you have a great opportunity to get your training off to a good start. This training will revolve around housebreaking (covered in the previous chapter), teaching commands, dealing with annoying puppy behaviors (like mouthing your hands and grabbing everything not nailed down to the floor), starting off-leash training, building your dog's confidence, and initiating street training.

Teaching Your Dog His Name

The first thing you need to teach your puppy or dog is to look at you when you say his name. This is easy to teach. Have a pocketful of treats. Wait until your dog is not looking at you. Call his name. When he looks at you, reward him. You can even throw the treat to him. He does not have to come to you. Do this in lots of different places and with increasing levels of distractions.

Teaching Commands: Sit, Stay, Okay, and No

Training to teach specific words should begin at about eight to nine weeks of age. This training will set the tone of your relationship right from the beginning. Your puppy will learn to enjoy training, and the positive nature of this training will counteract the effects of other corrections you will be making as you raise your puppy. Your puppy will also learn that you will be communicating with him with words and signals, and that he will be rewarded for paying attention and responding.

Start with a hungry, alert puppy and a lot of treats. These treats should be very small in size, so that your puppy will not get filled up quickly, and should be something soft that he can easily eat. Good examples would be hot dogs sliced into pieces the size of a nickel and then cut again into quarters, or semimoist cat treats. Start training in a place where your puppy will not be distracted.

You will immediately notice a benefit of using food: you have your puppy's attention! The first command you will teach is "sit." You can do this training either standing or kneeling beside your puppy. Your puppy will be standing, most likely dancing around trying to get at the food. Take a piece of food in your right hand and hold it so that it is almost touching your puppy's nose. For now, it is okay if he is chewing on your fingers. Say your dog's name to get his attention, then give the command to sit: "Max, sit." Say it in a pleasant tone of voice. Then move your right hand backward over your dog's head so he tips his head back and falls backward into a sitting position. If he doesn't sit right away, keep trying until he does. You shouldn't have to touch Max at all, but if you are really having problems, gently push his rump down with your left hand. Ignore any attempts Max makes to jump up and get the food, and don't give it to him until he sits with all four paws on the floor. He will soon figure out, without your punishing him, that jumping up won't get him the food. He will also be learning the hand signal to sit, which is the same hand motion you have been making, minus the food.

Soon your puppy will be following you around and sitting, as described in the first chapter.

Everyone in your family should learn how to do this, even young children. It helps to have kids keep the piece of food closed in a fist until the puppy sits, and then open their hands flat to give it to him. In this way, they won't get their fingers chewed.

The next exercise will teach your dog several things. In addition to teaching him the meaning of the words "stay," "no," and "okay," your puppy will be learning to accept restraint, a very important lesson.

Start this exercise by kneeling beside your puppy. Have two pieces of food in your hand. Tell him to sit, preferably on your left side, and make the hand signal he has already learned. Reward him with one piece of food. Then, while you restrain him with one hand, put a piece of food in front of him, about one foot away. It may be easier to have someone else place the food in front of him at first, so that your hands are free. In a firm tone of voice, tell him, "stay." Restrain him by placing your right hand on his chest and your left hand on his rump. You should be able to keep him in a sitting position this way.

If your puppy tries to get up before you say "okay," say, "No, sit." Some puppies may frantically struggle against the restraint. If your puppy does, give him a little shake while keeping your hands in place and say "no." There is no reason to become more forceful; simply be more stubborn than he is. When he gives up and stops struggling, say "okay" and release him, indicating to him that he can eat the piece of food on the ground, and praise him.

You want your puppy to understand that "no" means to stop doing whatever he is doing, and that "okay" means that he is released from the previous command. If you are going to teach your dog to stay, he has to have a word that means the end of the stay. For instance, you want to be able to tell your dog to stay when you open the car door and not get out until you say "okay." You don't want the release command to be "good dog" or a hand motion. You want to be able to praise your dog without releasing him. "Good dog" should mean "I like what you are doing; keep doing it." An example of this would be if your dog was lying down and staying while you had company. You would want to be able to praise him without having him get up. If you use some sort of movement to release your dog, then anytime you moved when he was staying, he would jump up.

Accepting restraint is important for dogs to learn. It is important not only for teaching them to stay, but also for accepting restraint when receiving veterinary care and grooming, and even accepting the restraint of a small child hugging them. Dogs who do not accept restraint often bite when restraint is attempted. A problem with restraint can mean that the veterinarian cannot draw a blood sample for a heartworm test or look at an infected ear. It can mean that a long-haired dog becomes a matted mess because he cannot be brushed. At its worst, it can result in a child with a scarred face

This puppy is learning to sit and stay. (Belgian Tervuren)

because she put her arms around a dog's neck and hugged him. Starting early with this simple exercise is a good way to prevent these problems.

Practice this exercise until your puppy will stay without your having to hold him in position. Gradually increase the length of time he will stay. Make him stay when you give him his dinner. Anyone who has had a dog jump up and hit a bowl full of dog food and send it flying all over the kitchen will appreciate the value of this training. Make your puppy stay until the bowl is on the floor, then wait a few seconds before you release him with an "okay" to eat his food. Again, every member of the family should be able to do this.

Once these two exercises are mastered, you can proceed with the rest of the training detailed in chapter 5.

An easy way to train a small dog is on a table.

Handling Puppy Behavior Problems the Positive Way

Puppies seem to be in perpetual trouble. One minute your little puppy terrorist is jumping up and biting at your hands while you are trying to read the
newspaper; a few minutes later you find him chewing on the fringe of the
Oriental carpet. Next he is racing through the house with one of the kids'
stuffed animals in his mouth, being chased by the tearful owner of the toy
and defying capture. Then he suddenly stops and relieves himself on the carpet. What do you do?

Punishment is not the answer. As annoying as all these behaviors are,
they are all normal puppy behaviors. It isn't fair to punish a puppy for engaging
in normal puppy behaviors before you have given him time to learn the rules
for living in human society. Punishment would only confuse him and make
him afraid of you. Remember, we are talking about a 7- to 12-week-old puppy.

The real answer requires understanding, prevention, training, and time.
Puppyhood is a temporary state. The razor-sharp needle teeth will fall out.
Your puppy will eventually have tasted everything in your house and will be
bored with it. He'll calm down, at least a little. He'll hopefully learn the
rules. Meanwhile, you want to prevent damage, distract him from getting
into trouble, and tire him out with plenty of exercise.

Mouthing upsets and scares many puppy owners because it seems aggressive. People expect a fuzzy bundle of love when they get a puppy, not a tiny
alligator with hair. However, mouthing is a perfectly normal puppy behavior.
It is how puppies and even adult dogs play with each other—they chew on
each other. So a puppy mouthing you is only attempting to play with you in

the way that is most natural to him. With age, the little needle teeth fall out, and with a little mild discouragement, the puppy learns that mouthing is not an acceptable form of play with humans. Many corrections that people make to try to solve this problem actually end up stimulating the puppy and making it worse. Very few dogs are still mouthing when they grow up, so don't kill yourself trying to correct a problem that will go away on its own. Your mouthy puppy is not trying to dominate you; he just needs to find a human-compatible way to play.

A dog who tends to mouth a lot and a small child can be a difficult combination. Puppies tend to view small kids as littermates and play with them accordingly. This can be very frightening to a child who is not much bigger than the dog. Try kneeling and fending off a rambunctious puppy from that height. It's not easy. Parents need to teach their children to behave appropriately around the puppy, such as not running through the house and roughhousing with the puppy. Parents also need to firmly discipline the puppy for nipping at the kids.

If things get so bad that your three-year-old is taking refuge from the puppy by climbing on the kitchen table, or your five-year-old's clothing is being torn, you need to take further action. Fill a spray bottle or plant mister with a 50-50 mixture of water and white distilled vinegar. Instruct your child to say "no" when the puppy grabs at him and then spray the puppy in his face. The vinegar will not hurt his eyes. Do not allow your child access to the spray bottle unless you are directly supervising him. The spray bottle will eliminate the chance of provoking a defensive reaction from the puppy. Never allow your child to hit your puppy.

Preventing damage is done by limiting your puppy's freedom. As with housebreaking, do not let him have free run of your home. Keep doors to rooms shut. Just as a baby might be put in a playpen for his own safety when he cannot be watched, confine your puppy when he cannot be watched. The use of crates and exercise pens is discussed in chapter 2. Teach your kids to pick up their toys and your husband to pick up his socks.

Damage control also means puppy-proofing your home. For example, to deal with a puppy who is chewing the fringe on the Oriental carpet, roll up the carpet and put it away until the puppy is older. You could also tuck the fringe under the carpet and tape it there. Another tactic would be to spray the fringe with something the puppy won't like the taste of, such as Grannick's Bitter Apple spray (available in dog supply stores and catalogs). Apply this kind of creative problem solving to whatever problems you are having.

When your puppy grabs something he shouldn't have and runs around the house with it, do not make the multiple mistakes of chasing him, wrestling whatever it is out of his mouth, and then punishing him. All these actions will make the problem worse. Chasing him is exactly what your puppy wants, so you are rewarding him and thus making it more likely that he will repeat the behavior in the future—exactly what you don't want.

You'll find him grabbing things just to get your attention. Instead, try to get him to come to you. It helps if your dog is trained to come when called, as described in chapter 6. You might want to wait a few seconds before calling him to give him a chance to discover that nobody is going to chase him. Don't use a threatening or angry tone of voice. Entice him to you with a treat if necessary, exchanging the treat for whatever he has in his mouth. This problem is especially difficult if you have young children who are all too anxious to join in the catch-me-if-you-can game. A family conference at which everyone promises not to chase the dog if he has something in his mouth is a good idea.

Trying to pull something out of your puppy's mouth is again rewarding a behavior you don't want. Just as playing chasing games is a normal puppy play behavior, so is playing tug-of-war, so these behaviors are easy to encourage unintentionally. Pulling on something will encourage him to hang on harder. To get your puppy to release something, apply pressure with your thumb and forefinger on both sides of your dog's muzzle, pressing his lips against his teeth. At the same time, give your dog the command "drop it." He will learn to drop things when you just touch the side of his mouth, and eventually on command. Don't forget to praise him for releasing the object.

Punishing your dog in this situation will only make him less likely to come to you next time. He will grab something, then run off and hide, where

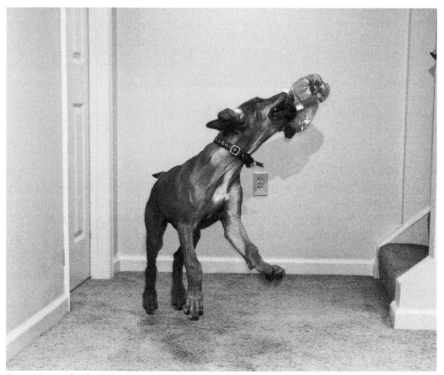

Sometimes the best toys are as simple as an empty soda bottle. (Rhodesian Ridgeback)

A game of tug is a good way to use up puppy energy and won't make your puppy aggressive. (Belgian Tervuren)

you won't discover he is destroying it until it is too late. If you cannot tell him "no" when he is thinking about grabbing something, it is too late to punish. See more about this in "Stealing" in chapter 8.

Tug-of-war is a good way to use up puppy energy, contrary to some myths about raising dogs. It is certainly a good alternative to having your puppy bite you or your clothing. You can use something as simple as the leg cut off an old pair of jeans. Dog sport competitors try to teach their dogs to play tug because it builds attention and relationships. Do not continue tug-of-war if your puppy plays too aggressively and gets too excited, although some playful growling is not a problem. Make sure your puppy will release whatever you are using on command. It's a good way to work on the "drop it" command. Give the command and stand very still, no longer tugging. As soon as your puppy lets go (which may take a while at first), reward with more tug play.

Distracting a puppy with lots of toys is a good technique to prevent damage and to use up puppy energy. Instead of giving him all the toys at once, try giving him only two toys at a time, then exchange them for two new ones when he becomes bored. Seven- to 12-week-old puppies need soft toys because they do not have adult teeth and will soon be losing their baby teeth. Toys that would be dangerous to give them as adult dogs are safe now, such as a piece of fake fur cloth that they can pretend to kill. Sometimes the best toys are as simple as a knotted rope, a cardboard paper towel roll, or an empty plastic bottle.

If prevention, distraction, calling your puppy's name, or using the command "leave it" (see chapter 5) don't work, you will have to do something physical to get your puppy's attention. Don't continue yelling or chasing your puppy. *Silently* approach your dog, take hold of his collar and give him a shake as you repeat the command. If he is up on a counter, grab him by the scruff of the neck and pull him off. Make sure he looks at you and he makes eye contact. You should be forceful enough to make your point, but not so much that your puppy avoids you.

Some puppies do bite aggressively, which is an entirely different matter than playful mouthing. If your puppy growls or snaps when you try to take something away from him, when you try to move him when he is sleeping, when you try to restrain him, or when a stranger tries to pet him, all these instances require immediate and very firm discipline as described above. Read more about aggression in chapter 9 and, if the biting continues, obtain the help of a dog trainer experienced in handling such problems.

Never hit your puppy with your hand or an object. It generally just causes your puppy to get more excited and may trigger a defensive response on his part if he interprets the hitting as an attack. Don't verbally abuse him, either. Loud screaming will undermine his trust in you.

Exercise is a great way of dealing with all puppy behavior problems. A tired puppy gets into less trouble. Puppies need frequent, short bursts of exercise. One way of tiring out a puppy is having two people stand 50 feet or more apart and call the puppy back and forth between them, giving the puppy a treat each time he comes. You will be teaching your puppy to come when called and tiring him out at the same time. We had fun with our Greyhound puppy by tying an old dust mop cover to a piece of string and letting her chase it. I'd hold her while my husband took off running, dragging the dust mop behind him. When he was far enough ahead, I'd release her to chase after him. The walks you will be taking as part of your off-leash training will also help. And one of the best ways to tire out a puppy is to give him a chance to play with another puppy.

Be realistic. Some damage is probably going to be done while you are raising a puppy, in spite of your best efforts to prevent it. A magazine may be ripped up, trash may be strewn all over the floor, and you may get a nasty scratch from puppy teeth. If you can't handle this without getting angry, think twice about bringing a puppy into your home. Even if you are looking at your most expensive pair of shoes in tatters on the floor, remember that he is just a puppy and try to laugh. Losing your temper is a waste of energy. It won't bring your shoes back. And remember, you left them where he could get at them.

Enjoy your puppy's antics. I laugh now at the memory of Zephyr, my Greyhound, who jumped in the car while I was unloading my groceries, grabbed a package of rolls, and took off through the woods at top speed, leaving a trail of rolls behind her. Although it may not seem so at the time, you'll miss the puppy games after they grow up.

Be realistic about the possibility of some damage occurring while raising a puppy. (Belgian Tervuren)

Building Confidence

Building your dog's confidence is an important part of getting off to a good start. Dogs start to develop their attitudes toward people and the outside world as soon as they can see and hear, so exposing a puppy to people and places to build his confidence around them, often called *socialization*, should begin as soon as you get him, ideally at 7 weeks. Your dog should be confident with people of all sizes and shapes and in new situations and places. If this exposure does not start before a dog is 12 weeks old, your dog may have confidence problems. He may be afraid of people or afraid when you take him to new places. He won't be happy, and neither will you.

Start by introducing your puppy to lots of different people—children and babies, tall people, fat people, men with beards, and women with large hats. He should meet these people both at your house and in other places.

If your puppy shows fear of anyone, be careful not to inadvertently praise him for being fearful. This happens when an owner tries to reassure a frightened puppy by petting him and speaking soothingly to him. Unfortunately, the puppy thinks that you are praising him for acting fearful and will act more fearful in the future. Fearful behavior can then progress to growling and snapping. Don't misinterpret this as overprotectiveness on the part of your dog. Your dog is simply afraid, and has been encouraged to act that way by you. The proper response to fearfulness is to insist your puppy not back away from whatever frightens him. The sit-stay (see chapter 5) is a useful tool in dealing with this situation. In a firm but kind voice, tell your dog to stop acting silly.

Expose your puppy to different people to build his confidence. (Belgian Tervuren)

Then have the person of whom your puppy is afraid offer him a bit of food. Try to make the puppy take a step forward to get the food. Then praise your dog for this behavior. If your puppy acts fearful of anything, don't avoid these situations or people with your puppy. Instead, try more exposure. Be careful, however, not to create such panic in your puppy that his fears are just further reinforced. You can push a little, but not too much.

A typical example is Tiki, a Yorkshire Terrier. Tiki was enrolled in my obedience classes when her biting problem worsened. This is not unusual in small dogs because it is easier to tolerate biting in them. When Tiki walked into the first class and I went to greet her, she hid behind her owner, who promptly picked her up and started cooing words of reassurance in Tiki's fringed ear. With that kind of backup, Tiki then turned into a miniature canine terrorist, snarling and growling at me. After I explained to Tiki's owner the effects of her reassurance, we started a program of building Tiki's confidence. I sat on the floor and offered Tiki, who was not in her owner's arms, a delectable tidbit of cooked beef liver seasoned with garlic powder. At first, she would only come as far as my outstretched arm. Gradually, I coaxed her closer, until she would finally climb into my lap. After a few weeks in class, we started to have the other class members offer Tiki a treat. We made sure Tiki was hungry and therefore motivated. It became a ritual after class; everyone fed Tiki before leaving. Meanwhile, Tiki was receiving the same treatment at home. By the end of the class, Tiki was running to greet people.

Some people are afraid to encourage friendliness in their dogs because they want their dogs to be protective. However, only a confident dog, a dog who is not afraid of people, can be counted on in a threatening situation. Socialization is absolutely necessary to help a dog distinguish between who is threatening and who is not. Protective behavior, if your dog has such instincts, will not emerge until your dog matures. If you see aggressive behavior in a puppy under six months of age, you can be sure it is caused by fear. Do something about it immediately.

Besides exposing your dog to different people to build his confidence, you will also want to take him to different places. Check with your veterinarian regarding when a puppy's vaccinations will provide him with adequate protection from infectious diseases. Meanwhile, take him to places where he won't be exposed to such diseases. City dogs should go to the country, and suburban dogs should visit the city. Don't just take him to outdoor places. Ask a good friend to let your puppy come inside his house—on leash, of course! If the weather is warm, puppies can learn to swim at 8 to 10 weeks of age. Take it slowly; wade into the water and support your puppy. Remember, the idea is to build his confidence, not to scare him.

A good rule of thumb is to expose your puppy to anything he may face in his life before he is 16 weeks old. Be creative. How about elevators, open staircases, wheelchairs, and baby strollers? An overnight stay at the boarding kennel where you plan to leave your dog when you go away is a good idea

Puppies should be exposed to children as early as possible. (Irish Setter)

while he's still a puppy. Your puppy should have a chance to interact with other dogs. Puppy training classes are an excellent way to provide your puppy with exposure to different people, dogs, and places. (For more information on choosing a good training class, see chapter 10.)

Taking the time to do this confidence building while your puppy is still young will give you many years of enjoying a confident dog. Your dog will be more adaptable and flexible. He will be better behaved when he meets new people or goes somewhere. If your dog is older, he will still benefit from such exposure, although progress may be slower.

Starting Off-Leash Training

Seven to 12 weeks of age is the perfect time to start your off-leash training. In fact, it is almost the only time. This time is so critical because during these weeks most puppies will instinctively stay close to their owners. After 12 weeks, dogs become more independent and more likely to stray.

Dogs not given the experience of off-leash freedom at this age will be much more difficult to train to obey when off leash later. By starting now, you can avoid the vicious cycle caused by lack of off-leash exercise. Dogs caught in this cycle build up energy and frustration, so they run away when they are finally off leash; this in turn makes it less likely that their owners will give them off-leash freedom, and the dog's frustration gets even worse.

It is best to never develop a dependence on the leash for control in the first place. While you should accustom your puppy to walking on leash, try to give him as much off-leash freedom as possible. If it isn't safe to allow your puppy to run free in your yard, take your puppy someplace where he can safely be off leash during this time period. Even if you have a fenced yard where your puppy can be off leash, you should still take him to someplace different, so you both get the feeling of off-leash freedom. Do this even if it means driving a distance. An advantage of going someplace different is that your puppy will naturally be more insecure and pay more attention to where you are. Just put your puppy down and start walking. Do not constantly call to him; you want to establish in him the habit of keeping track of where you are without your having to call him all the time. Several times during each walk, call your puppy to you, give him a treat, and turn him loose with an "okay" to run some more. Always carry treats with you when your puppy is being exercised off leash, so you can reward him for coming.

These off-leash walks will have a special effect on your relationship with your dog. They strengthen your emotional ties in a magical way. It is almost as if you are re-creating the times when wild canines struck off on the hunt together. In any case, there are few activities a dog enjoys more than a

Taking your young puppy for walks off leash is wonderful for getting your relationship off to a good start. (Basset Hound)

chance to be free to run and explore. Even if off-leash control is not important to you, I recommend these walks for the bond they create between you and your dog.

Once you've gotten your off-leash training off to a good start, continue teaching your puppy to come when called as described in chapters 5 and 6.

Dogs bred to hunt, like this German Shorthaired Pointer, need a lot of exercise.

4

Understanding Your Dog's Personality

To form a good relationship with your dog, you have to have two-way communication. The following chapter will be about training your dog to understand your language in the form of commands. First, however, you need to learn to understand your dog. This mutual understanding is critical for effective training and to establish a good relationship.

Personalities are what make dogs so fascinating, and they are all different. Each dog is unique. Your dog's personality will affect his training, so it is important to understand some of the factors that make up a dog's personality. Many of the factors are hereditary; as such, they cannot be easily changed and are best handled with a strong dose of understanding.

Behaviors Related to Breed

Most breeds were developed to do a specific job. An important part in understanding your dog is to research what job he was bred for and recognize how that affects his behavior as your pet. Although few purebred dogs are still performing whatever job they were bred to do, the behaviors remain. To confuse the issue, these behaviors remain in varying strength. An infamous example is the Irish Setter, who has been bred for beauty for so long that some have lost their ability to find birds. However, few seem to have lost their desire to run. Keep in mind as you are reading that these are generalizations that will not apply to all individuals within a breed.

Understanding how your dog's breed affects his behavior can be a challenge if your dog is a mixed breed. These dogs are often misunderstood because they don't have a breed identity to lead to an understanding of their behavior. Try to guess what breeds may be combined in your mixed-breed dog. Judge by characteristics like shape of ear, tail carriage, size, and coat rather than by color. Stick to the more popular breeds, as they are more likely to be part of a mixed breeding. It is unlikely that your dog is a cross between an Ibizan Hound and a Wirehaired Pointing Griffon.

Many breeds of dogs were developed to hunt in different ways that affect their behavior as pets. Some dogs hunt by sight, while others hunt by smell. Beagles, when off leash, are easily distracted by smells on the ground; Afghan Hounds are more likely to be distracted by something they see moving. Terriers were bred to hunt small rodents, which were sometimes not much smaller than they were. This produced a feisty dog who is eager to do battle and is not afraid of anything. Setters hunt by covering a lot of ground, and they will often do exactly that when allowed off leash.

An important factor that affects how easy it is to train your dog is whether or not his breed was developed to work in close cooperation with man or independently of him. For example, both the Golden Retriever and the Border Collie were bred to take directions from humans to do their job. On the other hand, when Beagles are working as hunters, they do not wait for instructions from their handlers, but strike off on their own, looking for rabbit scent. Setters and Pointers fall somewhere in between, searching independently for game birds, but staying within range of the hunter with whom they are working.

Some dogs were bred to hunt or work for long periods of time, such as Setters, Pointers, and Border Collies. You shouldn't be surprised if your German Shorthaired Pointer, bred to hunt all day at a steady gallop, paces restlessly around the house and gets into trouble when he doesn't get enough exercise. On the other hand, people are often surprised to learn that some of the breeds bred to hunt by running down game, such as Greyhounds and Afghans, are content to sleep away the day rather than run through the house. They were not bred to hunt all day at a steady pace, but to capture their prey in brief bursts of speed.

The behavior of dogs bred to herd, such as Collies and Shetland Sheepdogs, causes problems for many dog owners. It may mean that your Australian Shepherd obsessively rounds up the neighborhood kids in your backyard and won't allow them to move. Or it may mean that your Border Collie mix bites at the back of your legs when you try to walk. Herding breeds have an instinctive need to control moving objects. This works great if you have a herd of sheep you want to move, but poorly if the herding instinct is extended to small children or cars passing by. They are often compulsive retrievers, extending their herding instinct to balls or Frisbees. This herding behavior can be confused with an aggressive attack, and indeed the line between the two can sometimes be hard to draw. If you have a herding breed or mix, it would be wise to expose him to things like groups of small children running around and make sure he understands that under no circumstances is he to chase them.

These breed-related behaviors are instinctive, and they cannot be erased by training, only understood and controlled. Keep in mind that often these behaviors are at their worst in a bored dog. Terriers will dig, Huskies will howl, and Border Collies will chase cars. Training, stimulation, and exercise are all helpful.

Now we will examine some inherited personality characteristics that affect all dogs, regardless of breed. While we will be discussing extremes of each characteristic, there is a continuous range of behavior between the extremes that might best describe your dog. It is important to note that these personality traits are not necessarily good or bad, but rather a matter of personal preference. Puppy behavior testing gives a good indication of these personality traits at an early age (see chapter 3).

Evaluating Your Dog's Personality

Understanding your dog's personality is important for successful training and a good relationship. Circle the description below that best fits your dog.

Personality Traits	High	Medium	Low
Assertiveness	Barks or paws at door when wants to go out	Whines when his dinner is late	Rarely asks to go out or begs for food
Defense reaction	Readily bites when stressed	Would bite if very frightened	Wouldn't bite even if very frightened
Dependence	Very upset when left alone; never leaves your side	Unhappy when left alone; wanders away but not far	Would run away if given the chance
Energy level	Always on the move; needs lots of exercise	Likes exercise, but no problem if walk missed	Sleeps most of the time; couch potato
Reactivity	Gets excited easily; high strung	Gets excited when people come but settles down	Calm; laid-back
Intelligence	Is always one step ahead of you; easily bored	Learns quickly but isn't creative	Isn't quick to learn or solve problems
Trainability	Does whatever you want; easy to train	Has some bad habits but tries to please	Very difficult to train; independent and assertive

Assertive and Passive Dogs

If you have a dog who is somewhat of a "problem child," chances are that you have an assertive dog. Assertive dogs are those who actively try to get their own way. Because of this, they are more difficult to handle than a passive dog who is willing to be a follower. The passive dog does not take the initiative. He is not a creative thinker, as the assertive dog is. Assertive dogs are the ones who learn to ask to go out to relieve themselves, while passive dogs do not. They bark to make sure you don't forget to feed them dinner. And why is it that some dogs steal food at any opportunity, while others never do? Again, it's the difference between an assertive and passive dog, rather than a difference in appetites. The passive dog is one who is obedient, even though he's never had any formal training. The assertive dog, even if he holds several obedience titles, is rarely described as obedient.

Note that there is a difference between assertiveness and aggression. A dog can be assertive without being aggressive, and a dog can be aggressive without being assertive. For instance, Sandy is a mixed shepherd who snarls and snaps at anyone who approaches within five feet of her because she is afraid of people. She is a very timid dog who is scared of her own shadow. She is an aggressive dog, but she is certainly not assertive. On the other hand, Hayley is a Gordon Setter who is assertive, pawing at you constantly for attention and not taking no for an answer. She barks at the door when she wants to go out, which is approximately every 15 minutes. If all else fails, she will steal something she knows she is not supposed to have and will run through the house with it—a sure attention-getter. However, one cannot imagine any circumstance in which Hayley would bite.

My Borzoi, Carla, was the epitome of an assertive dog. What Carla wanted in life was more food, and she would go to any length to get it. She learned to open cabinet doors in the kitchen, so we put childproof locks on all those doors behind which food was kept. We live on the Appalachian Trail and are often visited by hikers. Carla learned to operate the zippers on their backpacks to steal their food. One of her more appalling stunts was the time she pushed open the door to a neighbor's home, walked in, stole a huge piece of Vermont cheddar cheese, and calmly strolled out, all while the dumbfounded neighbor looked on.

On the other hand, it would never enter Sabre's mind to jump up on a countertop and help himself to a piece of food, although he loves to eat just as much as Carla did and spent years watching her steal food. Sabre is a passive dog. We call him "The Boy Scout" because he never seems to do anything wrong. It isn't that he lies around the house doing nothing. He's a confident, energetic dog who is always ready for a game of Frisbee and is a great watchdog. He just doesn't take any initiative.

The passive dog is easier to live with, but there's a lot to be said for the surprises and entertainment an assertive dog can give you. Becoming equally assertive and developing a strong sense of humor may help you deal with this type of dog. Training is a must to set limits for the assertive dog, but don't expect to change his personality.

Aggressive or Passive Defense Reactions

Whether or not a dog tends to bite when he is frightened or stressed is an inherited behavior. While all dogs can bite if severely stressed, some dogs resort to biting more quickly than others. These are dogs with aggressive defense reactions.

The different types of defense reactions are easy to observe in my obedience classes during the class in which we teach toenail clipping because so many dogs are frightened or stressed by this procedure. A big male Golden Retriever may be totally terrified and struggling with all his might, but he does not bite. Meanwhile, an Airedale has bitten the hand of my assistant instructor for simply holding his paw.

These tendencies can be observed in puppies during puppy behavior testing at seven weeks of age when undergoing the restraint test. Puppies who are stressed by being held on their backs can react by freezing in fear or by the other extreme of growling and biting. However, some puppies are not stressed by being held on their backs and lie there quite relaxed, which brings up an important point. These puppies may or may not have aggressive defense reactions, but they are not easily stressed. Some dogs are more easily stressed than others, and this affects how easily a defense reaction of either type can be provoked. A dog with aggressive defense reactions who is easily stressed can be very difficult to handle.

Aggressive or passive defense reactions are linked to a dog's breed. Obviously, dogs bred to be protective, such as German Shepherds and Dobermans, are also bred to have aggressive defense reactions. Retrievers, on the other hand, are bred to have "soft mouths" so they won't crush the birds they were bred to retrieve, and consequently have passive defense reactions. Newfoundlands are another example of a breed that tends to have passive defense reactions. Unfortunately, the indiscriminate breeding of dogs has blurred many of these breed tendencies.

Dogs who show signs of aggressive defense reactions benefit from being trained as young as possible to accept restraint so they can be groomed and given veterinary care without biting. See chapters 3 and 5 for instructions on how to do this.

When training a dog with aggressive defense reflexes, any kind of punishment or force that makes the dog feel a need to defend himself must be avoided. You don't want to give the dog practice at biting by provoking such a reaction. On the other hand, dogs with passive reactions are often victims of forceful training techniques because they do not defend themselves. Food training works well for both types of dogs.

Defense reactions are an important personality factor to keep in mind when choosing a dog who will be around children. If you have small children, it is safest to have a dog with passive defense reactions.

Independent or Dependent

Dogs vary in how dependent they are on their human owners. Dogs are social animals, as are their wild counterparts, wolves. It is a dog's ability to form social attachments that makes him so desirable as a companion. All dogs need social contact to be happy, but some dogs are more stressed when denied that contact than others.

A gauge of a dog's independence is how he reacts to being left alone. The dependent dog is highly stressed in this situation and sometimes exhibits behavior problems such as barking, destructive chewing, and house soiling. He tries not to let you out of his sight when you are at home, following you from room to room.

The independent dog needs less human contact to be happy. He does not exhibit stress-related behavior when left alone, and while he is happy to see his owner return, he does not act as if he has been dying while his owner was gone. This is a useful trait for a dog who has to be left alone for long hours while his owners go to work.

Dependence is affected by both heredity and environmental factors. There are several different environmental factors. As a dog grows older, he usually becomes more independent. The presence of another dog provides social contact and decreases a dog's dependence on his owner.

A more complicated environmental factor revolves around the age at which a dog is removed from the litter. Dogs who are separated from their littermates before the age of six weeks are often more dependent, sometimes showing severe anxiety problems when separated from their owners. On the other hand, dogs who are not removed from the litter and exposed to human contact before 12 to 16 weeks of age may not bond well to a human and therefore may be more independent.

The hereditary nature of dependence is indicated by breed tendencies. As a general rule, hounds (both sight- and scenthounds), terriers, and the northern breeds are more independent. Chow Chows and Siberian Huskies are notorious examples of popular but independent breeds. Spaniels, retrievers, and herding breeds are more dependent. For instance, German Shepherds, Shetland Sheepdogs, and Golden Retrievers are examples of breeds generally having a dependent nature. Other breeds fall somewhere in between. When a breed was developed for doing a job that required submission to a human's direction, dependence was bred in as a desirable trait.

As with all personality traits, dependency affects training. Independence causes two main training problems. The first is that the independent dog is more difficult to motivate because he is not afraid of his owner's displeasure. In other words, he doesn't really care if he pleases his owner or not. While verbal praise may motivate a dependent dog to obey his owner's command, it will not be sufficient motivation for an independent dog. Food rewards are good motivation for independent dogs. The other common training problem with an independent dog is that off-leash control is difficult to establish because the independent dog has no natural inclination to stay close to his owner.

Puppy behavior testing gives a good indication of a dog's degree of dependency. Puppies who keep wandering away from the tester between and during tests are showing independence.

Energy Level and Reactivity

As an obedience instructor, I frequently get complaints about "hyper" dogs. I've learned that this means one of four things: a perfectly normal dog who doesn't get enough exercise, a dog who has a high energy level, a highly reactive dog, or a hyperactive dog.

The high-energy dog is always ready to go. He doesn't tire easily, whether he's working or playing. The highly reactive dog may or may not have a high energy level, but he reacts strongly to stimuli. Stimulation overexcites him. If you touch him, he jumps away. If the doorbell rings, he becomes hysterical. He startles easily. In an exciting or stressful situation, he may tremble. Such dogs are often described as "nervous" or "high strung." If you were to open an umbrella in the face of a highly reactive dog, he would startle and jump back. A dog with a low reactivity level wouldn't even blink an eye.

Both high-energy and highly reactive dogs benefit from training. For the high-energy dog, it helps to use up some of his energy. The highly reactive dog benefits from being taught to control his reactions. Repeated exposure to different people, things, noises, and places will reduce reactivity. Both types of dog also benefit from more exercise.

The hyperactive dog is different from both of these. Hyperactivity is a neurological disorder. These dogs cannot slow down. They tend to learn poorly due to an inability to pay attention for any length of time. They often have multiple behavior problems. Training and exercise do not help much with these dogs. As with hyperactive children, they can be treated with drugs. The drugs used are not tranquilizers. Some veterinarians do not have much experience with this problem. If you suspect your dog is hyperactive, you will probably need the help of someone specializing in dog behavior problems. Some owners have reported improvement with dietary changes, such as eliminating preservatives from the diet.

Intelligence and Trainability

Many dog owners are confused when their dogs seem to be intelligent but prove to be difficult to train. Intelligence and trainability are not the same thing. In fact, many dog trainers consider the more intelligent dog harder to train. Intelligence refers to a dog's ability to solve problems, while trainability is related to the ease with which a dog can be convinced to take direction from a human. A dog might use his intelligence to get what he wants, but he won't necessarily use it to do what you want.

It is interesting to note that most puppy behavior tests do not test for intelligence, but test more for factors that affect trainability. Being able to train a dog is more important to how people get along with their dogs than intelligence.

Maggie was a mixed Shepherd who displayed a mixture of intelligence, independence, and assertiveness that frustrated her owner. Maggie learned to open the latch on the back door to let herself out of the house. She learned to listen for when her owner was in the bathroom so she could raid the garbage can. To help get some control, Maggie's owner enrolled both of them in a local obedience class. Maggie quickly learned all the exercises—heeling, sit-stay, lying down on command. She learned just as quickly that she only had to do these things in the class because at home her owner didn't make her obey the commands. Maggie was certainly an intelligent dog, but trainable? Maggie's owner didn't think so.

What makes a dog trainable? Trainability depends on a combination of personality factors. The average pet owner finds a dependent, passive dog with a low to medium energy level, low reactivity, and passive defense reactions easiest to live with. A dependent personality is probably the most important factor, because it makes a dog anxious to seek your approval. Dogs are harder to train when they are assertive, are independent, have a high energy level, or are highly reactive. Nonetheless, any dog without a psychological disorder is trainable. The training techniques described in this book work for dogs of many different personalities. For instance, using food motivates independent dogs who are not motivated by praise as are more dependent dogs. Food rewards help keep the attention of a highly reactive dog, and they reduce the need for force that may induce an assertive dog with active defense reactions to bite.

While training some dogs is easier than others, training is unsuccessful only due to human error, such as failure to communicate what is wanted, failure to adequately motivate, inconsistency, lack of patience, or just plain giving up.

The intelligent dog may be great at solving problems, but may not be the easiest dog to live with. (English Springer Spaniel)

"Reading" Your Dog

Our dogs speak eloquently to us in a language of their own, a nonverbal language of body and face movements. You need to listen with your eyes to "read" your dog's body language. Understanding this language is essential for two-way communication, and therefore necessary to train your dog and to have a good relationship.

A good way to learn about dog body language is to observe dogs communicating with each other. Give your dog the opportunity to socialize with other dogs, and watch how they interact. How does he greet familiar dogs versus strange dogs? How does he get another dog to play? What games do they play? How do they behave when they get angry at each other?

Another way to learn about your dog's language is to read books on dog and wolf behavior. Since dog and wolf behaviors are similar, the interactions of wolves in the wild give scientists a chance to observe communication in a pure form, as it exists without human interference. For example, a dog behavior that many people find annoying is licking people's faces, especially their mouths. The origin of the behavior is rarely seen in dogs, but observations of wolves have shown that wolf puppies are fed by food that is regurgitated by older wolves. This regurgitation is triggered by the wolf pups jumping up and licking at the older wolves' mouths. In this way, wolves could bring home meat from their kills and have it already predigested for their puppies—wolf baby food. This is rarely observed in dogs because puppies are removed from their mothers shortly after weaning. The licking at mouths persists as a greeting behavior in wolves after they have matured. This is why your dog greets you by jumping up and trying to lick your mouth.

Mistakes in interpreting dog body language result in training errors. A common scenario of miscommunication takes place when an owner returns home to find that his dog has destroyed something in his absence. The owner acts angry, and his dog reacts by slinking with his eyes averted or by rolling over onto his side. The owner interprets this behavior to mean that the dog knows what he did wrong and feels guilty. The owner then proceeds to punish him. However, dogs instinctively react to threatening or angry behavior by acting submissively. For instance, my Greyhound acts submissively anytime I am mad, even if it is because I burned dinner or the car broke down. She certainly doesn't know why I am angry. In the case above, the dog is being punished without having the vaguest idea why. He may have committed the destruction minutes after his owner left, and is being punished eight hours later. This punishment will only serve to make him more anxious about his owner coming and going and more likely to react to this stress by destroying something the next time his owner leaves.

As a dog obedience instructor, I often find myself telling a student, "Your dog doesn't understand what you want." This is said to caution a student who is preparing to punish a dog for disobeying a command that the dog doesn't understand in the first place. Typically the disobedience is blamed on the dog's stubbornness. This is another example of how a training error can be committed by misreading a dog. Being able to tell the difference between when your dog is confused and when he is choosing not to obey is critical to good training. A dog's trust is destroyed when he doesn't know what to do to avoid punishment.

Reading your dog is an art. Your dog is already very good at reading you and understanding your emotions by observing your body language. He does it so well that at times he almost seems to read your mind. You owe it to your dog to try to become equally adept at reading him. Developing a friendship with your dog depends on it.

The Issue of Dominance

Many dog trainers believe that you must dominate your dog in order to successfully live with him. Obedience training classes ring with the cry, "You must dominate your dog!" and "You must be the pack leader, the alpha figure," a sentiment echoed in many dog training books. It is also claimed that if you don't dominate your dog, he will try to dominate you. Your dog is the enemy; obedience class is often the battleground.

I don't agree with this. You don't have to dominate your dog in order to train him and have a good relationship. The justification given for this insistence on dominance is that a dog's human family is a substitute for a dog pack, and that the social organization of dog packs, like wolf packs, is based on a dominance hierarchy. This dominance hierarchy is supposedly maintained by displays of dominance on the part of the pack leader. Therefore, the reasoning goes, human owners should be dominant over their dogs.

There are many problems with this line of reasoning. First of all, the outstanding characteristic of wolf and dog social behavior is the cooperation and friendliness among pack members, not their struggles for dominance. It is questionable whether the social order of wolves or dogs is based on dominance displays by one individual. Another problem is that dog and human combination "packs" are very different from wolf packs. Besides the obvious fact that there are two different species involved with all of the inherent communication difficulties, humans must control their dogs in ways that have no parallel among wolves. This reasoning is simplistic. The interrelationships of wolves in a pack, or dogs and their human owners, are complex and vary with the individual personalities involved.

For cooperative social groups to function, there have to be differences in personalities so dogs, wolves, or people can serve different functions. As we've previously seen, dogs are born with different personality traits. Just

One of the outstanding characteristics of wolf and dog social behavior is their friendliness toward each other.

The friendly social behavior of dogs comes to them from their wolf ancestry.

like people, some have more leadership qualities and some are content to be followers. It takes both to make a cooperative social group work. These differences mean that not all dogs want to take over the leadership position, just as it is true that not all people want to be leaders.

Rarely do dogs try to dominate their owners. A dog who doesn't do what the owner wants him to do is not necessarily trying to dominate his owner. Our dogs live in a world full of restraints that prevent them from behaving as they would like. It is natural that they will struggle against them. A dog pulling on the leash is not trying to dominate his owner. He simply wants to go faster or to be free, or maybe even enjoys pulling. Only when extreme assertiveness is combined with active defense reactions and no training do dogs behave in a manner that might be described as dominating their owners. Dominance aggression, when dogs bite their owners, is a separate behavior problem. See chapter 9 for more information on this.

Emphasis on dominance causes many problems in dog-human relationships. Domination can result in avoidance, fear, and suppression of a dog's initiative. It is possible to dominate a dog by suppressing undesirable behaviors with force while still not communicating to the dog what you want. Mutual communication is cut off when an owner fears that his dog is always trying to dominate him, and a dog's initiative to communicate is suppressed. Worst of all, establishing dominance is often used as an excuse for using unnecessary force in dog training.

Dog owners will improve their relationships with their dogs by placing emphasis on respect, clear communication, and mutual cooperation, rather than on dominance. The domestication of dogs has given us power over them by virtue of their dependence on us for survival. We must control our dogs for their safety and well-being, but we must be careful not to abuse this power. Instead, we should use this power in a positive way to allow our dogs to live a happy life and to give ourselves the full benefit of our relationship with dogs.

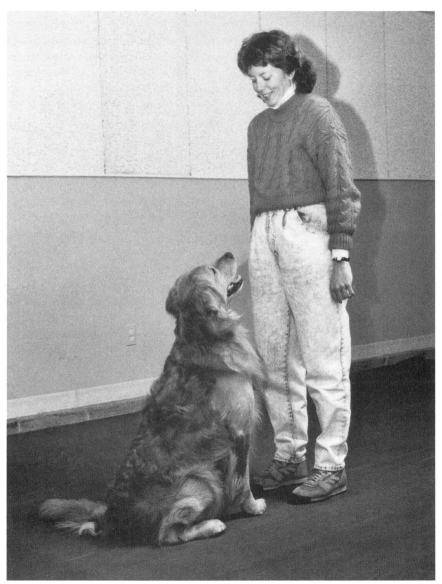

Eye contact is a special way to communicate with your dog. (Golden Retriever)

5

Basic Training the Positive Way

Basic training involves teaching your dog the meaning of commands and motivating your dog to follow them. You will be teaching your dog to sit, stay, come, walk on a leash without pulling, not jump up, leave it, accept restraint, lie down and stay, and stand and stay. This training can be done with a dog of any age, even an old dog, as long as he is healthy. Puppies can start learning a few easy exercises, like down and come, at 9 weeks of age. Most of the exercises below can be taught starting when the puppy is 12 weeks. Do not use any leash corrections until your puppy is over 16 weeks old.

Each command will be taught in several steps, and you can teach more than one command at a time. To help you plan your training, it has been broken down into five weekly assignments, with a test at the end to evaluate your progress. At the beginning of each week's lesson, there will be a list to summarize what you need to practice, followed by a detailed description of how to do it.

You should practice every day if possible, even if for only 5 minutes before you feed your dog. How long you should practice depends on your dog. Read your dog to tell when he has had enough. About 15 minutes is average, but a young puppy may not last that long, while a more exuberant dog may take 15 minutes just to settle down and begin concentrating. It is better to practice in two shorter sessions per day than one long one. Your dog's concentration span will get longer as training progresses.

The best way to practice is to include training in your everyday life. Practice down-stays during commercials while you are watching TV. Make your dog sit and stay while you put his food down. Practice walking on a loose leash every time you walk your dog. Stop along your walks and ask your dog to make eye contact and pay attention to you. Put your dog on leash and make him do a sit-stay when someone comes to visit. Make him do a sit-stay before you open the door to let him out.

Having the right equipment and treats will help make your training easier. Let's talk about what you will need.

Treats

The most important training tool you will use is treats. You'll need treats every time you train your dog, and lots of them! The treats should be something small because you don't want to have your dog's hunger run out before you are finished training. They should also be something that your dog doesn't need to chew a lot to swallow, so dog biscuits are usually a poor choice. What food you use depends on your dog and the situation. The less motivated your dog is by treats, or the more distracting the situation is, the more attractive or powerful the treats need to be. What works at home when no one else is around is not going to work when you are at obedience class with several other unfamiliar dogs, some of whom are barking.

Here are some typical treats and their power:

Low
- Dog biscuits
- Soft treats from the supermarket (check out the ingredients first!)
- Cheerios
- Pieces of a high quality dry dog food of a brand your dog doesn't usually eat
- Pieces of baby carrots

Medium
- Pieces of cheese (string cheese is convenient, or try a hard cheese, like Swiss)
- Pieces of hot dog (see recipe below to make them easier to handle)
- Pieces of semimoist cat treats
- Better-quality soft dog treats from a pet supply store

High
- Pepperoni
- Liverwurst
- Cooked beef liver
- Pieces of leftover pizza
- Steak or roast beef
- Cubes of hard salami
- Freeze-dried liver

Hot Dog Recipe

Use chicken or turkey hot dogs for lower fat. Cut two hot dogs in half lengthwise, then into nickel slices. Lay hot dog pieces on a napkin or paper towel on a microwave-safe or paper plate. Microwave on high for about three minutes. This will help cook out some of the fat as well as make them less slimy for easy handling.

Use low-power treats at home to reward behaviors your dog already knows. Use a medium-power treat to teach a new behavior when there are no distractions. When the distractions are high and it will be difficult to get your dog's attention, use high-power treats. Be sure to use very small pieces of food when training. They only have to be big enough for your dog to smell them: the size of a pea for medium and large dogs, smaller than that for small dogs.

Some of you may be thinking that your veterinarian said never to feed your dog people food. Veterinarians say this because they are concerned about your dog becoming overweight, and because some dogs have a reaction to having too much fat in their diets. Let's face it: dog food ingredients are often poor-quality people food, so your dog should not have a problem with digesting some of the more powerful treats I recommend. Just make sure that they only constitute a small percentage of your dog's diet.

Save your treats for training. Don't give your dog treats for no reason. They know you love them without the treats. Save any leftovers that you may normally give your dog after your meals for training, too.

A word to those of you who are saying that your dog isn't motivated by treats. If your dog is healthy, this probably means that you are overfeeding him. If your dog doesn't finish his food in under three minutes, you are probably overfeeding him. Dog fat doesn't jiggle. An overweight dog looks like a sausage, without a waist and like his skin is stuffed tight. Your dog, no matter what the breed, should have an indentation at his waist when you look from above. Ribs should be easy to feel.

Another thing to keep in mind is that the recommended amounts of food on the back of a dog food bag are designed to sell dog food. I have yet to meet a dog who can consume these amounts. Don't be surprised to find that your dog only needs one-half to two-thirds of the amount listed, especially if you are using treats. Do not allow your dog to pick at a bowl of dry food all day long. You cannot control his weight that way, and he will never be motivated for training. Even worse, you will miss that early warning sign of a sick dog: a skipped meal.

This dog is fat. (Labrador Retriever)

This dog is at an ideal weight. (Labrador Retriever)

To keep your food treats quickly accessible, it is helpful to have some sort of small bag or pouch that you can attach to your waist. An easy way to make one is to cut the back pocket off an old pair of jeans, leaving about two inches of material above the pocket. You can then pin this to your waist in front of you with a large safety pin. There are also treat pouches available in pet supply stores and catalogs.

Collars

Your basic training collar will be a buckle or quick-snap collar. Every dog should have one. You will attach any tags and identification. This is the only collar that is safe to leave on your dog when he is alone. Try to do as much of your training as possible on this collar.

A disadvantage of buckle collars is that some dogs can back out of them. This is dangerous if you are walking on a street. For this situation, I recommend a martingale type collar. A popular brand is a Premier collar. This type of collar closes enough to prevent your dog from escaping, but not enough to choke your dog.

When it comes to teaching your dog not to pull on leash, you may find it useful to use something other than a buckle collar. There are several to choose from, all of which work by making your dog uncomfortable when he pulls.

My favorite is a head collar. Some popular brands are the Gentle Leader and Halti. Head collars work by pulling a dog's head to the side when he pulls forward. These are very humane and the most effective way to stop pulling on leash. Head collars have a strap that goes around a dog's neck and another that goes around his muzzle. They work like a halter does on a horse. If a halter can control a thousand-pound animal, it can control the largest Newfoundland, the most headstrong Lab, or the most stubborn terrier. Head collars are great for working with dogs who lunge for any reason, whether to jump on people or chase squirrels, or because of aggression problems. They can make trips to the vet much less stressful.

Prong collar, nylon choke collar, buckle collar, martingale collar.

A Gentle Leader head collar. (Great Dane)

The main disadvantage of the head collar is that it can be hard for a dog to adjust to having something on his face. Dogs sometimes paw at their faces initially, trying to get the head collar off. They may even throw themselves on the ground. Most dogs, however, adjust quickly, especially with treats to help. Sometimes the dogs who need it the most object to it the most, so give it a chance. I love seeing the smile on an owner's face at the instantaneous and miraculous cure for a dog's pulling problem.

The other disadvantage of head collars is that other people may think your dog is wearing a muzzle and is aggressive, although this is becoming less of a problem as the popularity of head collars increases. A dog can eat, drink, and even bite with it on. One caution: do not use head collars with a long line or retractable leash. A dog could hit the end of a long leash with too much speed and hurt his neck.

When using a head collar, it is very important to release all tension on the leash the instant your dog stops pulling. That is your dog's reward. Don't keep constant tension on the leash. This can be a hard habit for you to break if you have had to keep a death grip on your leash to hold your dog. If your dog continues to dislike the head collar, it is probably because you are keeping it tight all the time.

If your dog is not a bad puller and has no aggression problems, you may want to try a pinch or prong collar. This collar looks like a horrifying instrument of torture, and that is exactly how I thought of it for years before trying it and discovering otherwise. I first used one on a student's dog in desperation. Why two little old ladies had adopted a Saint Bernard cross from the local Humane Society was beyond my understanding, but they did. The first

What Kind of Collar Should You Use?

Type Of Collar	Advantages	Disadvantages
Buckle Collar	Cannot choke dog Easy to put on Safe to wear at most times	Dog can escape from Gives minimal control
Martingale Collar	Cannot strangle dog Dog cannot escape from Safe to wear at most times Easy to put on	Only minimal help for pulling
Choke Collar	Dog cannot escape from When used with jerks, offers better control	Dog can strangle Requires training Can only be worn during training Requires physical strength Will injure a dog's neck with repeated use
Prong Collar	Gives more control Does not choke dog Requires less strength	Looks cruel Harder to put on Can only be worn during training Can increase aggression
Head Collar	Gives instant control Requires no training Requires no strength Prevents pulling without causing pain	Looks like a muzzle Harder to put on Some dogs object to initially
No Pull Harness	Stops pulling	No steering Harder to put on
Harness	Will not hurt dog's neck	Encourages pulling No control over dog's attention Harder to put on

All collars, head collars, and harnesses require a proper fit.

night of obedience classes, my husband had to go out to their car to bring the dog in. I needed to find an easy way for them to control the dog, or he most likely faced euthanasia. Finding a home for this monster-sized dog would have been next to impossible. So I tried a prong collar. It worked beautifully. Much to my surprise, the dog did not scream with pain. He learned to walk on a leash.

Your dog's temperament determines whether the prong collar is appropriate for him. If your dog is easily stressed, is nervous, or tends to be aggressive, a prong collar is not for him. The discomfort he may feel may make him too excited. A prong collar is also not a good training tool for someone who loses his temper easily. Be honest with yourself about this for your dog's sake.

There are special harnesses to reduce pulling on leash that work by pulling on the sensitive area under a dog's front legs. These work, but it can be hard to steer a dog with a harness.

My least favorite collar is a choke collar. It is difficult for people to remember how to put them on properly. It is the collar that is most likely to kill your dog if he is left unattended. If you use it effectively by jerking your dog's neck, you can damage his neck. Without these jerks, a choke collar is ineffective, as your dog will continue to pull and gag. Prong collars are more effective than choke collars and less damaging, and cannot strangle your dog.

Clickers

A clicker is a little mechanical device that makes a clicking noise when you push it. It is becoming a popular tool for positive reinforcement training. Your dog is taught to associate the sound of the clicker with treats, and then the unique sound of the clicker clearly tells your dog when he is right. In technical terms, the clicker is a "conditioned reinforcer," a sound previously meaningless to your dog that becomes meaningful when associated with food or some other reward. (Also see chapter 1, "Other Rewards.") Conditioned reinforcers are how dolphins and killer whales are trained, since a trainer

This is a clicker.

can't be right beside them to reward them. A dolphin performs a behavior like jumping through a hoop. The conditioned reinforcer, perhaps a whistle, is given during the jump. Then, the dolphin swims to the side of the pool to get his fish. Conditioned reinforcers, like clickers, bridge the gap between the behavior and the delivery of the reward. When you click *during* (not after!) the behavior you want, it is like taking a picture of the behavior and marking it exactly for the dog. Clicker training is a great way to communicate to your dog.

Clicking can speed up training because it is a fast, precise, unique sound. Praise words, like "good," are also conditioned reinforcers, but words can get lost in all of the other words we say as we talk to our dogs. The advantage of clickers if that they force us to concentrate on what our dogs are doing right, rather than waiting for them to be wrong and then correcting them. *It is always better training to catch your dog in the act of being right, and then reward him.*

Electronic Shock Collars

These collars are used to punish dogs. Don't be misled by descriptions that the collars work by administering "stimulation" to your dog. They give your dog a shock. As I wrote in the first chapter of this book, punishment has many disadvantages. There are two types of problems that I hear from people who try them. The first is that if a dog doesn't know what to do to stop the punishment, he will become frightened and depressed from a sense of help-lessness. The pain may increase anxiety and aggression, making the behavior problem worse.

The other problem is that the dog will become frightened of everything associated with the pain. I've seen dogs who are afraid to go outside because that is where they were first shocked. Think about what kind of housebreaking problems this can cause! Timing is critical in using punishment, a skill that can take years of dog training experience to develop. For this collar to be effective, your dog must have completely learned a behavior and have had tens of thousands of repetitions. People who buy these collars as short-cuts to training will likely waste their money and cause mental damage to their dogs.

My strong advice: **Do Not Use Electronic Collars.**

Citronella Spray Remote Collars

I do like citronella spray collars in some circumstances. They work by having a puff of citronella spray come from a box on a collar that hits under a dog's chin. They startle a dog rather than really hurt him. There are fewer side effects with good results. However, the same criticisms apply as do to electronic collars. A sensitive dog can become fearful. For the collar to work, a dog must have thoroughly learned a behavior through thousands of repetitions with positive reinforcement.

Leashes

Your basic training leash should be four to six feet long and made of leather, nylon, or cotton webbing. Make sure your leash is lightweight enough with a small bolt snap for small dogs. Likewise, there is no need for a bolt snap big enough to hold a horse to be on the end of the leash, no matter how big your dog is. Too large a snap could hurt your dog's eye.

Retractable leashes are very useful. They give your dog more freedom, when it is appropriate, while avoiding tangling around a dog's leg. I find mine especially useful when I am traveling with my dog. They are great for leash breaking puppies and for working on the come command.

Another useful leash is a slip lead. This is a leash and collar in one. I keep one by the door so I'm always ready to prevent jumping up when someone comes to the door. It's easier to slip over a dog's head when the dog is excited than to search for a ring on a collar to which to attach a leash.

Most of the training that follows in this chapter should be done on a four- to six-foot leash.

Basic Training Skills

First, a word about commands. When you train, commands are usually accompanied by body motions. Your dog is better at reading body language than understanding separate words because he doesn't naturally communicate with words. Because of this, he will pick up on body signals faster than

A retractable leash gives your dog the freedom of a longer leash while eliminating the problem or tangling. (Shetland Sheepdog)

A slip lead is convenient for preventing jumping up when kept by the door.

word signals. That's okay. It is important that you are aware of this so that you are not frustrated when he doesn't respond to the word alone. He will also pay more attention to the inflection you use when you give a command than the individual word. Words are hard for dogs to learn because they do not talk!

You can help your dog learn commands more easily if you are consistent in your choice of words. Just think how you would feel if you were learning a foreign language, and instead of teaching you one word at a time, someone kept giving you five different synonyms for the same thing. Instead of just learning "friend," one day you heard "friend," and the next day "comrade," and the next day "companion," "buddy," and "chum." This is how your dog feels when he hears "come," "come here," "here," and "get over here." So stick to one word and use it consistently. Make sure everyone in your family uses the same word, too.

When you give a command involving movement, it is usually best to say your dog's name first, to get his attention, and then give him the word signal, or command. Realize that this is the opposite of how we normally talk. We usually say, "How are you, John?" We put the person's name at the *end* of the sentence. Be conscious of this so that you are careful to always say your dog's name before the appropriate command, not after. Give your commands in a friendly but firm tone of voice. There's no need to be loud, either. If your dog can hear the sound of a box of dog treats being opened when he is three rooms away, he can hear you speaking in a normal tone of voice.

Don't worry about using a command when you are beginning to teach your dog a behavior. It is best to first teach a behavior using a piece of food

Ten Rules for Good Training

1. If you are in a bad mood or irritated at someone, don't train your dog. It will be too tempting to take it out on your dog.
2. If your dog is too full of energy to concentrate, exercise him before training.
3. Make sure your dog is hungry when you start training.
4. If you feel yourself losing your temper, stop training.
5. Read your dog carefully so you know when he is becoming stressed. Signs of stress might be looking away from you, partially closing his eyes, a droopy tail, lips pressed tightly together, and trying to get away from you. If you see these signs, back up and make the exercise easier.
6. If you are having trouble with one part of the training, move on to something else and come back to the trouble spot later.
7. Be more stubborn than your dog is.
8. Be 100 percent sure that your dog understands what you want before assuming he is choosing not to obey you.
9. Pay as much attention to your dog as you expect him to pay to you.
10. Always end your practice session by playing with your dog for a few minutes.

Go get your dog, and let's get started!

to lure your dog into the desired position, then to attach a command to the behavior once your dog can do it. There is no reason to repeat, "Max, down," while you are trying to lure your dog into a down position for the first time. Your dog won't know what "down" means, and you'll be distracting him with your voice. Wait until your dog is reliably lying down; then, add a command to it.

The order in which you give praise and food treats is important, too. In chapter 1 under "Other Rewards," it was explained that by giving the praise *before* the food treat, the praise becomes a conditioned reward. Remember, too, that praise is important as reassurance for your dog. Read this section in chapter 1 again before beginning training. Also remember that praise, such as "good dog," is used differently from the release word "okay." If you need to review this idea, see chapter 3 under "Teaching Commands: Sit, Stay, Okay, and No."

Whenever you are teaching your dog a new command, the training should be done in a place where your dog (and you) won't be distracted. Whenever possible, start the training indoors. Make sure you are the only person in the room. Once your dog is responding well, gradually add distractions and try the same exercise outdoors. Your goal is to have your dog respond to commands anywhere and under any conditions. You will have to practice in many places and with all the distractions of everyday life to achieve this.

A part of reading your dog that will improve your training is being able to anticipate when your dog is going to make a mistake, and preventing it from happening. For example, when your dog is on a sit-stay, you want to correct him when he thinks about getting up, not after he has already gotten up and walked a few steps away. Your dog will give you signs that he is about to get up. He might get restless and make small movements, like picking up a paw. He might look around. Then, right before he gets up, he has to shift his weight forward. This is the time to caution him to stay, saying, "No, stay," in a firm tone of voice. You have to pay close attention to your dog to read him in a situation like this.

Training Plans Week by Week

Week 1

Review responding to name
Review sit and sit-stay for food
Sitting on command without food in your hand
Sit-stay longer
Sit-stay at your side with distractions
Sit-stay for petting
Sit-stay with eye contact
Downing on command
Come and sit

Review Responding to Name

For instructions on how to teach this, see chapter 3 under "Teaching Your Dog His Name."

Review Sit and Sit-Stay for Food

For instructions on how to teach this, see chapter 3 under "Teaching Commands: Sit, Stay, Okay, and No."

Sitting on Command without Food in Your Hand

This is a simple but important exercise. Previously, you have always had a piece of food in your hand when you asked your dog to sit. Now you are going to ask your dog to sit without having the food in your hand, although you will still use food as a reward. To understand the significance of this step, you need to understand the difference between a lure and a reward. When food is used as a lure, it is shown to the dog *before* the dog responds. When food is used as a reward, it is not shown to the dog until *after* the dog responds.

You may have trouble making the transition between using the food as a lure and using it as a reward because your dog may not respond at first if he thinks the food is unavailable. Be patient. The first time you ask your dog to sit without the food in your hand, make the exact same hand motion as you did when you had food. This then becomes your sit hand signal. When your dog sits, reach into your pocket or a nearby container to reward your dog with a piece of food.

Sit-Stay Longer

To get a longer stay, you will now reward your dog while he is staying, instead of after you release him.

Sit your dog, tell him to stay, and place four pieces of food in front of him. Instead of releasing him to get the food, pick up one piece of food and give it to him while he is staying. Repeat this until you use up the food. Then release your dog with an "okay." If your dog breaks the stay, grab all of the food and remove it. Start over.

Your dog does not need another reward after being released. After all, the behavior we want to teach is stay, not to get up!

Sit-Stay at Your Side with Distractions

When you ask your dog to sit and stay in everyday life, he won't always be in a quiet room by himself. You want to teach him to stay in distracting circumstances.

Start with your dog sitting at your side on leash. Don't forget to reward or at least praise him for sitting. Tell him to stay as you give him the stay hand signal. Then bring on the distractions. Start with ones that are not difficult for your dog to resist, then build up to the harder ones. Distractions can be as simple as someone walking in a circle around you and your dog. Harder ones are someone running by, riding a bicycle by, or throwing a ball past you. This is the time to teach your dog to control his instinct to chase things, which often leads dogs into streets where they are killed. A challenging distraction in our classes is Mr. Spider, a windup cat toy that bounces and spins wildly across the room. If you have children, challenge them to come up with distractions. The rules are that they can do anything they want, except call your dog's name and touch him.

An Irish Setter displays good attention during a sit-stay distraction.

If your dog continually gets up, keep sitting him again and again until he stays. There is no need to use more force; just be more stubborn than he is. If you initially have to hold him in place, do it. When he does stay, praise, reward, and release.

Sit-Stay for Petting

Do you have problems with your dog jumping up? This is the problem people list most often on the registration form for my classes. Here is how you start solving that problem.

Doing a sit-stay for petting is just like doing any other sit-stay with distractions. Again, start with your dog sitting in heel position, and then have someone approach and pet him while you keep him sitting. Start with someone familiar to your dog, so he will be less excited. If he can't remain sitting while someone is approaching, don't let them pet him until he can do it. Your helper may have to approach your dog several times until he settles down and stays. Keep at it until he relaxes. The next time you practice, it should take fewer approaches to get him to stay. Don't forget to make him stay until you release him with "okay."

Sit-Stay with Eye Contact

It is impossible to communicate with your dog, or with another person for that matter, unless you have his attention. Teaching your dog to make eye contact is teaching your dog to look at you when you are speaking to him, a necessary foundation for all training.

Start by sitting your dog in front of you, facing you, and telling him to stay. Take a piece of food and move it slowly from in front of your dog's nose up to the bridge of your nose, between your eyes. As you are moving the food, give your dog a command ("Max, watch"). If your dog breaks his sit-stay or jumps up to grab the food, sit him again and start over. When your dog makes eye contact, praise him quietly, give him the food you had been holding up to your eyes, and release.

When your dog has caught on to the idea, ask him to watch for a gradually increasing length of time. Start by asking him to watch while you silently count to five. If your dog looks away and breaks eye contact, move the food back to his nose to get his attention and start over. Don't ask for more than 10 seconds this week.

It has been said that the eyes are the window to the soul. Nowhere is this more true than with dogs. Dogs say so much with their eyes. There is more to this exercise than just getting your dog's attention. It is a special way to make contact with your dog. Not only are you getting your dog's attention, you are also giving him yours. It is a mutual sharing. Whenever you are with your dog, try to make eye contact. When you do, smile at him. That is an easy way to express love.

Downing on Command

Good news. Teaching your dog to lie down on command is fairly easy. Sit your dog on your left side, and kneel beside him. No leash is necessary. Place your left hand lightly on your dog's rump so that he cannot stand up. Have a piece of food in your right hand. Hold the food near your dog's nose and use it like a magnet to draw your dog to the floor. Move the food straight down to in front of his toes. If you move it too far forward, he will stand up. As soon as his elbows touch the floor, pop the food into his mouth. Some dogs learn faster on a slippery surface; others are encouraged by a soft surface to lie down. Don't try to get him to stay down at this point. You only want to teach him to lie down. Add the command "Max, down" when he is doing the behavior readily.

Use food as a magnet to pull your dog into a down position. (English Springer Spaniel)

Come and Sit

The purpose of this exercise is to teach your dog the meaning of the word "come." It is the first of many steps in teaching your dog to come. The reason you are teaching your dog to sit in front of you is so that you can easily reach down and restrain him. Many people lunge and grab their dogs when they get close, inadvertently teaching their dogs to play keep away. Have you ever seen an owner and dog playing this game? The owner stands very still, hardly breathing, waiting for his dog to come close enough to be grabbed. When the dog gets close enough, the owner lunges. Since dogs have a well-developed ability to perceive movement, they see the grab coming and dart away. Then the game starts over, with the owner waiting frustrating amounts of time for their dog to come close again. Teaching your dog to come and sit can prevent this.

Begin teaching this exercise indoors. Start with your dog sitting in front of you. Since he is inside, he doesn't need to be on leash. Hold both your hands in front of you with a piece of food in them, at your dog's nose level. Give your dog a command to come in an inviting tone of voice. Back up quickly about four steps. Backing away takes advantage of your dog's instinct to chase. Use the food as a magnet to keep your dog in front of you. As you stop, bring the food up to signal your dog to sit and give the sit command. You should give the sit command and signal a moment before you stop so that your dog has time to slow down. Praise, reward, and release. Do *not* touch your dog to get him to sit. You will know he is getting the idea when he sits automatically without your having to tell him.

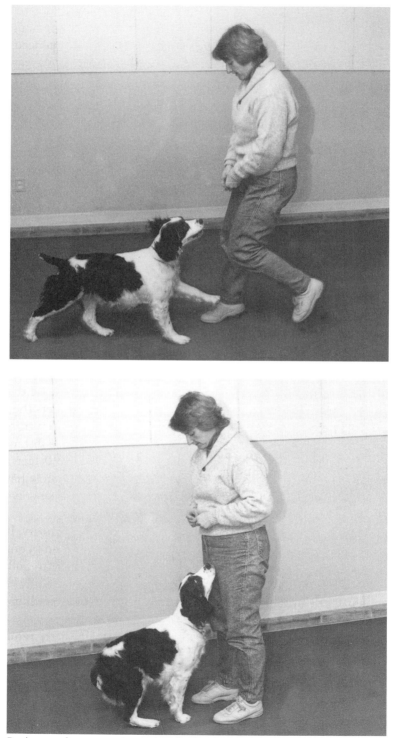

Back away from your dog, using the food as a magnet to keep your dog in front of you. (English Springer Spaniel)

After a few steps, stop and bring the food up to signal your dog to sit as you give the sit command. Once your dog is doing this well in the house, try it outdoors. Of course, have your dog on leash if you are in an unfenced area, but try to keep the leash loose. Don't use it to guide the dog in any way. You want the food, not the leash, to control your dog.

Week 2

Sit-stay while you move

Sit-stay away from home

Attention without food in your hands

Downing without food in your hand

Come and take hold of the collar

Come from a distance

"Leave it": Introduction

Walking on a loose leash: Part I

Sit-Stay While You Move

Do this on leash first. Sit your dog by your side, and tell him to stay. Toss a treat about two feet away. Repeat the stay command, drop the leash, and take a step away from your dog to pick up the treat. Return to your dog and give him the treat while he is staying. Release. Gradually increase the distance you throw the treat and walk away from him. When he gets the idea, stop throwing the treat. Take one step away from your dog. Return to his side immediately and reward. Once again, gradually increase the distance.

Even though dogs have to stay while their owners go 30 feet away and even out of sight in dog shows, in everyday life, you will rarely have to go far away. What you will have to concentrate on is a good sit-stay with distractions.

You can repeat the hand signal and stay command as necessary. If you repeat the command, you may want to omit his name, so he isn't confused and doesn't think you want him to come to you. Be careful not to pull him with the leash by mistake and cause him to move. Read him carefully so you can anticipate any moves and remind him to stay. If he moves, put him back into the place he was originally, and start over.

After you have reached the end of the leash, immediately return to him. Go all the way back to heel position, where you started. Do *not* call him to you. Calling him out of a stay will confuse him at this point. He will anticipate your call and will keep getting up to come to you. Make him stay until you are all the way back in heel position, and then praise, reward, and release. Gradually increase the amount of time he will stay at the end of the leash to one minute. It will probably take two weeks to get up to one minute.

Sit-Stay Away from Home

By now, your dog should be doing the sit-stay in heel position at home very reliably. You are probably still working on steadiness with distractions. Now you want to teach your dog that he has to listen to your commands away from home, too. When you are working away from home, start with things he knows well. It is normal to have to backtrack a little. Take him with you when you run an errand, like a trip to the post office, and just quickly get him out of the car and make him do a sit-stay in heel position. Try to find a place away from home, both indoors and outdoors, where you can practice this. Do you have an understanding friend or relative who wouldn't mind if you practiced inside their home? Don't forget to bring your treats to reward him and help keep his attention in a distracting situation.

Attention without Food in Your Hands

Just as when teaching your dog to sit on command without food in your hand, this exercise makes the same transition from using the food as a lure to using the food as a reward. First, warm up by doing the eye contact exercise as you practiced it last week, with the food in your hands. After one or two repetitions, bring the index finger of your right hand up to the corner of your right eye, without food in either hand, and tell your dog to watch ("Max, watch"). If he makes eye contact, praise him and reward him with a treat. If you're having difficulty, try touching him on his nose or the side of his face to get his attention, and then bringing your finger up to your eye. Be patient as you make this transition, and be quick to reward even a glance.

Downing without Food in Your Hand

Downing your dog without food in your hand is another transition from lure to reward. By making this transition, your dog won't be dependent on seeing the food first before obeying.

Warm him up by asking him to down a few times with food in your hand. Remember, you are not asking him to stay at this point. When he is downing well with the food, try one without. Have a treat in the nonsignal hand behind your back. Simply make the exact same hand movement you made when you had food. You can give a verbal command at the same time. As soon as his elbows touch the ground, bring out the treat from behind your back and give it to him.

Come and Take Hold of the Collar

This exercise is the same as the come and sit exercise from last week, except this time when your dog sits, you are going to reach down and take hold of his collar before you praise and reward him. You want to make sure he is comfortable with this motion and that he won't jump away. Have the food in your right hand, so that your left hand is free to take hold of the collar. Give your dog the food while you are still holding on to the collar. Remember, the sequence is:

1. "Max, come," as you back away.
2. "Max, sit," as you stop.
3. Take hold of the collar.
4. Praise.
5. Reward.
6. Release with "okay."

As your dog becomes more comfortable with this, you may want to reach and grab faster, as you might in an emergency, to accustom him to this. You should also practice calling your dog to you and snapping on the leash before praising him and giving him his reward.

Come from a Distance

Until now when you practiced the come and sit, your dog has been in front of you. Now you want to add some distance. There are several ways to do this. One is to call your dog to you when he is in another room. Make sure you have a treat available at least three-quarters of the time to reward him.

Another way to practice this is to have someone hold your dog while you go 5 to 10 feet away and call him. Give him the sit command before he gets to you so that he has time to slow down. The idea is *not* to have your dog run at you full speed, crash into you, and then sit down. Gradually increase the distance between you and your helper.

A good way to practice this if you have other people in your household is to call the dog from one person to another. If there are three people, they can form a triangle to practice. For your dog's own safety, he should respond to a come command from any member of your family. Everyone's command will sound different to him because of different voices, so he has to get used to all of them. Even children as young as three or four years old can participate in this exercise. This is a fun game for everyone. Once your dog gets the idea, he will start to race to the next person without a command! It's a great way to exercise a dog.

"Leave it": Introduction

This command means "don't touch" and is incredibly useful. You say it to your dog *before* he grabs something he shouldn't have, whether it is a towel in the kitchen, a bowl of popcorn on the coffee table, or a squished squirrel on the road that you find when going for a walk. Start by holding a treat closed in your fist. Hold your fist out to your dog. Ignore any attempts he makes to get it, like biting and pawing. When he gives up, even if for a second, open your fist and give him the treat. Then, add the command "leave it" when he is readily leaving your hand alone.

Walking on a Loose Leash: Introduction

Teaching your dog to walk on a loose leash without pulling means that you can give your dog (and you!) enough exercise, socialize him to the outside world, and spend quality time with him—all very important to making friends with your dog. We're not talking here about the stylized, precise heeling that you see in a show ring. We want your dog to stay on one side of you within a four-foot circle without pulling. You can use a "heel" command, if that is what you are comfortable with, or you can use "walk." Actually, you shouldn't have to use any command; your dog should automatically not pull.

There are collars that can help teach your dog not to pull on leash. Please see the section on "Collars" previously in this chapter for more information on that.

This can take a while to teach, so be patient, persistent, and positive.

Walking on a Loose Leash: Part I

In order to not pull on leash, your dog will have to pay attention to where you are. Let's teach that first. As always, we will show our dogs what we want them to do before training them what we don't want them to do. Treats will show your dog in a positive way where you want him to be.

Hold your leash in one hand and about five pieces of food in the other. Hold your leash in your left hand and food in your right, or vice versa, whatever is more comfortable for you. Hold the food close to your dog's nose, using it like a magnet to keep your dog by your side. Give your dog a piece of food every two to three steps. Try to keep walking as you do it. This will be awkward at first, but with practice, you'll get better at getting the food in your dog's mouth, and he'll learn to eat while he is walking. When your food runs out, release him, praise, and start over.

One of the easiest ways to start is with a long-handled plastic cooking spoon. Spread squeeze cheese from a can or peanut butter from a tube onto the spoon. Hold your leash in your right hand and the spoon in your left. Your dog will learn to lick and walk at the same time. This technique saves your back if you have a little dog. It also prevents your dog from nibbling too hard on your fingers, and you won't keep dropping treats on the ground.

Keep talking to your dog in a happy tone of voice to help keep his attention.

Use food as a magnet to keep your dog by your side. (German Shepherd)

Week 3

Attention with no hand signal

Walking on a loose leash: Part II

Using your leash to get your dog's attention

"Leave it": Don't touch things on the ground

Come away from distractions

Down-stay

Attention with No Hand Signal

This exercise has two purposes: (1) to teach your dog to look at you with a verbal command only and no hand signal; and (2) to further educate you and your dog in the use of food as a reward rather than as a lure. When you finish teaching your dog this exercise, you should have a better understanding of how positive reinforcement works. This is hard for your dog to understand, so practice in a quiet area initially.

First, warm up with last week's eye contact exercise by telling your dog to watch, then pointing to your eyes, without food in your hands. When he makes eye contact, praise, reward, and release.

When you are successful at that, try telling him to watch while your hands are hanging at your sides. You can even put them behind your back. There should be no food in them. If he looks up and makes eye contact, reward him with a piece of food. If he doesn't, keep talking to him softly or make kissing noises. The second he looks up, immediately stuff food in his mouth. Once he understands what you want, try to extend the amount of time he holds eye contact before you reward him. Don't ask him to hold it for longer than a count of five.

Walking on a Loose Leash: Part II

One of the reasons dogs pull is that it works; pulling makes you move in the direction they want to go. Dogs are rewarded for pulling. This week you are going to take away that reward. From now on, if your dog pulls, your goal is not to move forward. You can do this on a buckle collar.

Start by setting a very attractive and visible object about 30 feet away. It has to be something your dog will pull toward. This could be a bowl of food, a toy, or another person. Hold your leash about three feet from the snap. Start walking toward the object of attraction (OOA). The second your dog hits the end of the leash, start backing up away from the object. Do not turn around. Do not let your leash slip through your hands. Tie a knot in it if necessary. Keep backing up until your dog turns around and looks at you, and the leash becomes loose. Reward, and then start walking toward the OOA again. It is normal to go only one step at first. Be persistent, and when your dog finally gets close to the OOA on a loose leash, release him with an "okay" to go to it. You can also set a goal to cover a certain distance without your dog pulling, like down the length of the driveway. Same rules apply: back up until your leash is loose, then go forward again.

You won't be able to teach your dog to walk nicely on leash if you let him pull on leash sometimes and not at others. Consistency is critical for success.

Using a spoon spread with food is a convenient way to teach walking beside you. (Pug)

Using Your Leash to Get Your Dog's Attention

There will be times when you need to use a jerk on the leash to get your dog's attention away from distractions. A leash correction should be a sharp tug on the leash rather than a steady pull that your dog can resist. Do not do this unless you are sure that your dog understands what the commands mean through previous positive reinforcement training. It is not good for your dog's neck, so if you have to do it often, reduce the distractions, get better treats, and use a more effective collar.

"Leave It": Don't Touch Things on the Ground

Set up three distracting objects on the ground about 25 feet apart. These can be bowls of very attractive food (think liverwurst) or your children's dirty socks. In my obedience classes, we use paper plates full of horse manure. This really motivates my students to work on "leave it," especially when I remind them that their dogs will be kissing them later. Start with your dog on leash and lots of treats. As soon as your dog focuses on the distraction, and preferably before he even starts to pull toward it, give your dog the command "leave it." Use quick tugs on the leash to get his attention, and keep walking. When your dog finally looks away from the distraction and back at you, praise and give him a treat.

Keep going until your dog will walk by the distractions without even looking at them. Keep praising and rewarding!

Use your "leave it" command when your dog becomes glued to an interesting smell on a walk.

Come Away from Distractions

Distractions are the main reason that dogs do not come when called. If your dog doesn't come away from distractions when he is on leash, it is obviously unlikely that he will do so when off leash. This training is very similar to the "leave it" training. You may want to set up some distractions ahead of time. Litter your yard or practice area with things that will distract your dog. Good things might be a closed plastic container with food in it, or an unopened package of dog treats. You could pour melted butter on the ground so he will sniff. When things are set up, go get your dog and put him on leash. Have a treat handy to reward him, but don't let him see it; otherwise, he may not want to leave you. Let him wander around until he spots the distraction. Follow him around and keep the leash loose. When he is busy investigating, call him ("Max, come"). If he doesn't come, give the leash a quick tug, back up a few steps as you did when you were initially teaching him to come, and guide him into a sit as you stop. Even though he didn't come on his own, you should still praise and reward him for coming. Start to praise him the second he turns away from the distraction and comes toward you. Do not drag him all the way to you on a tight leash; just give him a tug to get him started. It is okay if he picks up the distracting article and brings it to you.

If your dog does come when you call him, celebrate! Praise him for a solid minute and reward him with four or five pieces of food. When your dog is good on a 6-foot leash, advance to a long line of 30 feet. Let him drag the line without you holding it.

You can practice this anytime you walk your dog. If he is sniffing the place where every neighborhood dog lifts his leg, or if he is straining at the end of the leash toward the neighbor's cat, call him, give him a tug, and back up.

Down-Stay

The down-stay is one of the most useful commands you can teach your dog. You shouldn't have to set aside a special time to do this. Anytime you are sitting down, perhaps watching TV, is fine. Start this training in a quiet, nondistracting situation to encourage your dog to relax.

Teaching the down-stay will be the same as teaching the sit-stay. Start with several pieces of food in your hand. Down your dog using one piece of food and give it to him. Tell him to stay. Put three or four pieces of food an arm's length away. Give him the food quickly, one piece after another, as he is lying down. If he gets up, pick up all the food and start over. Gradually lengthen the amount of time between pieces of food until your dog is staying three minutes.

Week 4

Stay without food

Attention: Look at you, not the food

Stand

"Off": Don't jump up

"Leave it": No stealing

Loose leash walking: Combining the parts

Restraint

Handling paws on a down-stay

Stay without Food

Now your dog needs to learn to stay without pieces of food in front of him. Don't move to this step unless you have done lots of practice with food in front of him. Start by making the stays shorter and with fewer distractions. If your dog moves, put him back in position without using food. There's no need to be terribly physical here. Just be more stubborn than he is. When he is successful at staying, reward him while he is sitting or lying down, and release him. Is it a problem if your dog lies down when you have left him sitting? No. That is only important if you plan to show your dog in obedience.

Attention: Look at You, Not the Food

When you are using food to train your dog, it is helpful to teach your dog that he should look at you and pay attention to you, not the food. Sit your dog in front of you, as in previous eye contact exercises. Have a piece of food in each hand, closed in a fist. Hold your fists at your sides. Your dog should know you have food in your hands. Give him a watch command. More than likely, he will stare at your hands and nudge at them with his nose. Ignore this. Keep giving him the watch command, softly calling his name or making funny noises. Hopefully, he will eventually glance at your face. When he does, give him one of the pieces of food in your hands. Repeat until he instantly looks at you and away from the food when he hears his name.

Stand

As I was writing this chapter, I decided I needed a break and took my dogs for a short walk in the woods behind my house. (Actually, it was my dogs who decided I needed a break.) They started a major excavation project in search of a chipmunk that had gone underground. When I ended their game, they were both covered with mud. We all returned home, and I was faced with the problem of muddy feet and light beige carpets. Obedience training to the rescue! I told the dogs to stand and stay while I dunked their feet in a bucket of water and then wiped them off.

The stand-stay is useful in many ways: for veterinary examinations, for grooming, as part of learning not to jump up, and of course, for wiping muddy feet. Start by sitting your dog in heel position. If you have a small or medium-sized dog, kneel beside him. Do this off leash, so that both hands are free. Take a piece of food in your right hand. Hold it close to your dog's nose. Move your hand away from his nose and parallel to the ground. With a big dog, you may have to take a step forward. This hand motion will become a hand signal to stand. Encourage him to stand up by slipping your left hand under his belly and lifting him to his feet. As soon as he stands up, give him the food, release him ("okay"), and praise. Do not try to make him stay at first. As always, add the command ("Max, stand") later.

There is another method for getting your dog in a standing position when you don't have food. Start in the same position, with your dog on your left side, kneeling if necessary. With your right hand, grasp your dog's collar under his chin. As you give your command to stand, pull your dog forward into a standing position. As with the above method, use your left hand under his belly to encourage him to stand.

The most common error people make in training their dog to stand is to pull up on the collar in a motion similar to the one used to sit a dog, so the dog is confused. Be careful not to do this. The difference is that to sit a dog, you hold the collar on top of the dog's neck, and pull up and back. To stand a dog, you hold the collar underneath the chin, and pull parallel to the ground.

Teaching your dog to stand-stay will make it easier for your veterinarian to examine him. (German Shorthaired Pointer)

"Off": Don't Jump Up

The command "off" means *don't touch with your front paws*. In other words, don't jump up. Before you correct your dog for jumping up, be sure that you have done thousands of repetitions of having him sit for a treat, with you and especially with other people. You will also need your dog to be able to do a sit-stay while someone walks around him. Start by having something that will entice your dog to jump up, such as a toy or treat. If he sits immediately, great! You've done your homework. If not, let him jump up as much as he wants and ignore him. As soon as all four feet are on the ground, give him the toy or treat. Once he is automatically staying on the ground, add the command "off."

Another way to teach "off" is with the leash. As someone approaches, warn your dog with the "off" command. If he launches himself into the air, give him a quick tug on the leash. Tell the person who is helping you not to pet your dog until he is sitting or all four feet are on the floor. You can also use "off" to correct your dog for jumping up on counters or furniture. Don't use the word "down" to mean no jumping. You have already trained him that "down" means something else. See chapter 8 for more information on dealing with jumping up problems.

"Leave It": No Stealing

There is another use for your "leave it" command. You already taught your dog not to grab things off the ground. Now you will use it to prevent him from stealing things off tables or counters. To practice, put something tempting on a table. A peanut butter sandwich close to the edge of the table would be good.

Pretend you are not paying attention. Tell him to "leave it." If he does not, you can correct him in a number of ways. You can just grab him by his collar and pull him away. If you don't think you'll be quick enough to do this, let him drag his leash. You can also use a spray bottle filled with half water and half white distilled vinegar. If he tries to grab the sandwich, spray him in the face. When your dog backs away and possibly sits, reward him with a low-level treat, like a dog biscuit. The spray bottle is a great tool for "counter surfing" dogs or dogs who jump up while you are eating.

Loose Leash Walking: Combining the Parts

When you go for a walk now, combine all of your skills for loose leash walking. Make sure you have your treats with you. If your dog pulls, back up or stand still until he loosens the leash. Be more stubborn than he is.

Use your "leave it" command when you are walking and your dog is about to lunge at something, like a cat or another dog. Tell him to "leave it" before he lunges. If he looks at you, praise and reward enthusiastically. If not, try a leash correction. If he doesn't respond to that, turn and walk in the other direction. Keep going until your dog gives up and looks away. Reward and try again. You can also use the spray bottle in this situation. Be patient, and don't lose your temper! However, don't be afraid to be firm.

Also, use the leave it command if your dog tries to stop and sniff when you don't want him to. Walks are for giving you and your dog exercise, so no stopping for sniffing.

Don't forget the most important thing: reward your dog often when he is walking nicely on leash. He doesn't have to be looking at you.

In my obedience classes, the test for loose leash walking is to be able to walk around my training school with your leash tied to the collar with a thread. If the thread breaks, you don't pass!

Praise, Practice, Persistence, and Positive Reinforcement all combine to teach your dog to walk on a loose leash.

Restraint

The importance of a dog accepting restraint was discussed in chapter 3 under "Teaching Commands: Sit, Stay, Okay and No." This exercise will further develop your dog's ability to accept restraint, this time in a lying down position.

Sit your dog in heel position, and kneel beside him. Have him lie down. Once your dog is down, gently roll him over onto his side. Press his head down flat against the floor. Tell him to stay and repeat the command as necessary. Hold him there with one hand on his neck and one on his hindquarters. When he relaxes, you can just quietly pet him as he lies there. Gradually work up to having your dog stay in this position for one minute. Release him with an "okay" and give him a reward. This is easy to practice while you are watching TV.

Teaching your dog to accept restraint can prevent aggressive behavior when your dog is groomed, examined by a veterinarian, or hugged by a child. (English Springer Spaniel)

Some dogs may strenuously resist doing this. It is important to be more stubborn than your dog is. He may even be frightened. If he is, it is important for him to learn that he will not be hurt, so don't give up. If your dog struggles strongly, it may be helpful to try a different position. Kneel so that your dog's back is against your knees and his legs are facing away from you when he is on his side. Hold the front and back legs that are closest to the ground. Hold your dog in this position until he relaxes. When he does, praise him quietly, release, and reward.

If at any point in doing this, you think your dog might bite you, stop immediately and seek the help of an experienced dog trainer.

Handling Paws on a Down-Stay

Next week you will be clipping your dog's toenails as part of his training to accept restraint. To prepare for that, here is a warm-up exercise. Down your dog and roll him over onto his side. Then handle each of his paws. Squeeze them as firmly as you will when you cut his toenails. Release him with an "okay" and reward him.

If you have already tried unsuccessfully to cut your dog's toenails, you may have to overcome toenail clipper phobia. Start by placing the toenail clippers by your dog's bowl when you feed him. Then put your dog on a sit-stay and reward him for staying while you hold the clippers in your hand. When he is comfortable with this, progress to putting him on a down-stay and touch his toes with the clippers. Be generous with your rewards.

Week 5

>Reliable sit
>Stay in the car and at the door
>Sit-stay for ear cleaning and teeth exam
>Stand-stay for petting and grooming
>Down-stay away from home
>Toenail clipping

Reliable Sit

There are times that your dog will ignore your sit command because he is very distracted or because you do not have a treat. When this happens, gradually pull up on the leash or collar until your dog feels discomfort but his front feet are still firmly on the ground. Keep the tension on until your dog sits. Do not jerk and release. The second your dog starts to sit, release the tension.

Your dog may take quite a long time to sit the first time you try it because he will not understand what to do to make the discomfort go away. Keep repeating the sit command in a calm voice. Be persistent (have I said this before?). Eventually it will take less tension and less time to get a sit, until you will only have to touch the collar. Remember to keep praising and rewarding with treats! (I think I've said this before, too.)

Stay in the Car and at the Door

For any of this training to be useful, it has to be incorporated into your everyday life with your dog. Using the sit-stay when you get out of the car and at doors in your house are examples of training exercises becoming an integral part of your life. Training exercises isolate what you are trying to teach your dog in situations where you and your dog can concentrate.

These stay exercises are important in protecting your dog's life. Dogs who bolt through doors, be they car doors or house doors, are endangering their lives. The time to teach your dog to stay at doors is not when you are in a hurry to go somewhere, but when you can concentrate on training your dog.

Your dog should stay while you get out of the car, open the back door, attach a leash to his collar, and give him the "okay" command. It may be helpful when you first try this to have his leash already attached to his collar. He does not need to sit first, but if you think that will help, go ahead and make him sit. Tell him to stay before you open your car door. If he leaps into the front seat and tramples you in an attempt to exit, close the door before he can escape, somehow get him into the backseat, and start over. Be stubborn. If he leaps out the back door before you give him the "okay," put him back in the car and make him do a sit-stay with the car door open.

You should also be able to tell your dog to stay and then open any door in the house without having him bolt through. Make it easy at first by doing this when your dog has just been exercised and is tired. You can do this on leash, placing your dog in a sit-stay a few feet from the door. Open the door slowly. If your dog gets up, slam the door shut, put him back in a sit, and start over. Be sure to have the treats ready to reward him when he gets it right.

Teaching a dog to stay when you open a door can save his life. (Shetland Sheepdog)

Once your dog is doing this well, attempt it when someone is outside knocking on the door. This will be a real challenge, but wouldn't it be great if your dog behaved in a somewhat civilized manner when people came to the house?

Have a family member or friend help you—someone who won't mind knocking on the door several times and having the door slammed in his face. When your helper knocks, follow your dog to the door, put his leash on, and tell him to sit and stay. This alone may be a challenge, so don't progress any further until you get this part under control. Then open the door. As before, if your dog moves, shut the door without allowing your helper to enter, and start over. Your goal is to have your dog stay while you open the door, the helper enters, you shut the door, and you say "okay." Have your helper come and go several times in a practice session, so that your dog gets used to it, is less excited, and has more chance of being successful. Put this training to use whenever someone comes to your house. Have your dog on leash before you open the door.

Sit-Stay for Ear Cleaning and Teeth Exam

This is a continuation of our exercises to teach your dog to accept restraint and prevent aggressive responses. When I think of this exercise, I remember a dog in my obedience classes who had a problem with this. Buffy was a difficult-to-handle Cocker Spaniel who was being trained by a 13-year-old girl. Buffy's ears were not kept clean, in spite of a Cocker's predisposition to ear problems because he struggled so much when he was restrained. Partway through the class, he developed a severe ear infection. A trip to the veterinarian resulted in a major battle in order to examine Buffy. Putting in the necessary daily eardrops was next to impossible, which prolonged the infection. After his ears finally cleared up, Buffy returned to class. When his owner reached down to pet his head, Buffy bit her, badly frightening her. A reluctance to be restrained had progressed to aggression. All this could have been prevented with training.

To clean your dog's ears, use a cotton ball or a tissue wrapped around your finger. Use a cleanser designed especially for a dog's ears that you can purchase at a pet supply store, from a catalog, or at your veterinarian's. It should be just for cleansing and not be medicated. I like the convenience of ear wipes, which are premoistened pads. You will be safe from reaching the ear drum if you remember to keep your dog's ears pulled straight up as you clean them. Of course, check with your veterinarian if you notice an odor or discharge, or if you need a demonstration of ear cleaning technique.

If you encounter problems with this, start by just handling your dog's ear and putting your finger in his ear. Be stubborn in insisting he stay sitting. Reward when you are successful. Then try just touching his head with the moistened cotton ball or gauze. Some dogs will be frightened by the smell. Work at just touching your dog's head until he is comfortable with it. Then move on to cleaning his ear. Remember Buffy, and don't give up.

Your dog should also allow his teeth to be examined. As dogs are living to an older age with better veterinary care, they have more dental problems. To examine your dog's teeth, start by putting him on a sit-stay. Then close his mouth and gently lift his upper lip up and back. Check the health of his gums as well as his teeth. He should not break his sit-stay.

Stand-Stay for Petting and Grooming

Once your dog knows the stand command, it is time to add the stay to the stand.

Have two pieces of food in your right hand. Kneel beside him, especially if he is small. Use one piece of food to lure him into a standing position. Give him one treat. Keep him standing, and place the second treat an arm's length away as you tell him to stay. When he has stayed for a second, pick up the food and give it to him while he is staying. Praise and release. This is just like the way you taught him to do a sit-stay, so he may be confused at first and keep sitting. Be patient. Keeping your hand under his belly at first will prevent him from sitting.

Once he can stand and stay, introduce petting and grooming. When you first ask someone to pet him, kneel beside your dog and have your hands on his collar and stomach to steady him. Have a treat out in front of him to give him something to focus on. Have your helper just touch his head. Build up to having him stand for a thorough body examination, running your hands down his back and legs, without your having to hold him. Brush him when he is in a stand-stay and insist he stay. And don't forget to use your stand-stay when at the veterinarian. He or she will be very appreciative!

Down-Stay Away from Home

It is easy to take your dog places with you if he can be put on a down-stay anywhere. You have practiced a down-stay at home with distractions, so this week try it somewhere away from home. A park or a friend's house would be perfect. Do you take your kids to baseball or soccer practice? Take your dog along and make him do a down-stay. Again, be stubborn. He probably won't cooperate at first, so just keep putting him down until he relaxes and stays. It is not unreasonable to ask him to do a down-stay for half an hour, or even longer. One of my introductions to dog training was when I was in college and took my Irish Setter to classes with me, in spite of signs on the doors prohibiting dogs in the buildings. We got away with it because Shauna did an excellent down-stay that lasted the 50 minutes of class. Dogs love to go places, and down-stay training will make that possible.

Toenail Clipping

Toenail clipping is an essential part of keeping a dog well groomed. It is a procedure that is often ignored by many dog owners. If your dog's toenails click when he walks across a hard surface, they are too long. He should not be walking on his toenails; that is bad for your dog's feet. Because a dog's toe-nails should be cut every two to four weeks, it is impractical to let this go until a groomer or veterinarian can do it.

Toenail clipping is also an excellent test of your dog's ability to accept restraint. It teaches a dog to tolerate something unpleasant but necessary, a part of many medical treatments. Such training enabled my husband, who is a physician, to stitch up one of our dogs in an emergency situation without anes-thesia. A dog who was visiting attacked my Borzoi over a food bowl, lacerating her face, with some of the cuts very close to her eyes. Unfortunately, this hap-pened during a terrible blizzard. It was impossible to get to a veterinarian. Carla cooperated by lying on her side very still while Brad stitched up her face.

Start by downing your dog and laying him on his side. In grasping his paw, be careful not to pull his leg into an unnatural position or get such a death grip on his paw that you are hurting him. If he struggles, do not get someone else to help you hold him. The idea is not to physically hold him in place, but to have training hold him in place. If he struggles too much, go back to last week's lesson and practice some more. Until he gets comfortable with this, you may be able to cut only one toenail at a time. This helps limit the stress for both the owner and dog. A good way to help hold your dog in position and make toenail clipping a positive experience is to use squeeze cheese or peanut butter in a tube. Someone else will have to help you with this. Let your dog lick the cheese or peanut butter as your helper squeezes out small amounts. Then you can clip his nails while he is distracted. You can also spread some of these treats on a spoon for your dog to lick. A friend of mine even puts a big glob on her refrigerator for her dog to lick as she clips.

Toenail clipping is an essential part of keeping your dog well groomed. (Greyhound)

The dotted line indicates the proper place to cut the toenail.

If your dog has light-colored nails, you're lucky. It is easy to see where the quick ends and where to cut. If your dog has dark nails, you will have to guess. The quick generally ends where the nail starts to curve down. Don't panic if you cut a little too much and your dog starts to bleed. If you don't overreact, he won't. Apply some pressure on the nail with a paper towel until the bleeding stops. It is helpful to have on hand a special styptic powder made to stop bleeding toenails.

Training Plan Summary

Week 1

Review responding to name and sit-stay in chapter 3
Sitting on command without food in your hand
Sit-stay longer
Sit-stay at your side with distractions
Sit-stay for petting
Sit-stay with eye contact
Downing on command
Come and sit

Week 2

Sit-stay while you move

Sit-stay away from home

Attention without food in your hands

Downing without food in your hand

Come and take hold of collar

Come from a distance

"Leave it": Introduction

Walking on a loose leash: Part I

Week 3

Attention with no hand signal

Walking on a loose leash: Part II

Using your leash to get your dog's attention

"Leave it": Don't touch things on the ground

Come away from distractions

Down-stay

Week 4

Stay without food

Attention: Look at you, not the food

Stand

"Off": Don't jump up

"Leave it": No stealing

Loose leash walking: Combining the parts

Restraint

Handling paws on a down-stay

Week 5

Reliable sit

Stay in the car and at the door

Sit-stay for ear cleaning and teeth exam

Stand stay for petting and grooming

Down-stay away from home

Toenail clipping

The Test

This test is designed to evaluate the progress you have made with your dog's training. The goal of passing this test will help provide you with motivation to train. If you can't pass all the tests, keep practicing until you can.

To get a more objective evaluation, give a copy of the test to a friend or relative so that they can score you. You may not have food in your hands during any of the tests, but you may have it in your pockets to use as a reward. Try to do as much as possible off leash. Remember to use your watch command if you are having trouble getting your dog's attention. If you pass, celebrate—pizza for both you and your dog!

The Training Test

Test	Excellent	Fair	Needs Work
Sitting on command	Sits with one command and hand signal	Command and signal need to be repeated	Will not sit without being touched
Attention to name	Looks at you immediately when hears name	Needs extra commands to pay attention	Does not look at you
Sit for petting	Stays with one command and waits for "okay"	Needs many commands to stay; gets up but doesn't jump up	Jumps up
Lying down	Lies down with one command and hand signal	Needs more than one command	Will not lie down without being touched
Heeling on a thread*	Heels without many commands or signals	Need lots of commands	Breaks thread
Come and sit	Comes on first command and sits	Needs lots of commands to come	Does not come
Down-stay for one minute	Stays down without many extra commands	Needs lots of reminds to stay; gets up but lies back down with minimum of effort	Gets up more than once

* Attach your dog's leash to his collar with a thread, or you can run his collar through a rubber band and attach the leash to the rubber band.

Training Never Ends

The more you train your dog, the better your relationship will be. The five weeks of training described in this chapter provide only a foundation that should be built upon with further training. Five weeks is enough time for your dog to begin to understand what the commands mean, but it is not enough time to achieve any degree of reliability. For response to commands and signals to become a habit, especially without food, it takes a thousand repetitions. You also need lots of practice in different situations, and different places, both indoors and outdoors. In order for your dog to retain what he has learned, you must continue training him throughout his lifetime. This reasoning is based on the principle that any learned behavior that is not reinforced will fade or deteriorate. What this means is that if you stop making your dog obey your commands and stop rewarding him for doing so, he will gradually stop obeying them. For instance, if you keep calling your dog to you and never reward him, he will stop coming; if you allow your dog to break a stay without correcting him, he will stop staying.

Training your dog for the rest of his life is not as much work as it may sound because you can and should include your training in your everyday life. This means giving your dog an occasional food reward for the rest of his life. It is not necessary or desirable to ever completely eliminate food rewards for your dog. If you don't keep giving occasional rewards, you will find yourself needing to punish him more to get him to listen to your commands. It would be better to prevent this from happening. These rewards do not have to be given every time. In fact, psychologists feel that rewards given irregularly make a behavior stronger.

Call your dog in a happy tone of voice. (Belgian Tervuren)

Never forget to reward your dog for responding to your commands. (Belgian Tervuren)

There are many more commands your dog can learn that would make your relationship with him more enjoyable. Teaching your dog to retrieve on command and deliver to hand is a good example. While such training is not necessary to live with your dog, it sure makes playing with him a lot more fun. Such additional training is beyond the scope of this book, but you can pursue it by reading more books or attending obedience classes. Finding a good class is discussed in chapter 10.

Remember the four P's of dog training: Practice, Persistence, Praise, and Positive Reinforcement!

6

Coming When Called and the Off-Leash Dog

Coming when called is every dog owner's dream, and most dog owners' nemesis. Yet it is so important to the quality of a dog's life, to a dog's safety, and to a happy relationship between dog and owner. Breathes there a dog owner who has not experienced the horror of chasing a runaway dog? You are filled with anger that it is happening, frustration at your inability to capture an animal who runs faster than you can, and fear that your dog will run out into the street and be hit by a car. Yet some of the biggest pleasures of dog ownership are based on a dog who comes when called off leash—playing Frisbee, going for a quiet walk in the woods or throwing sticks into a pond for your dog to retrieve. What a contrast of scenes, and it is all dependent on whether or not your dog comes when called.

Realistic Expectations

Training your dog to come when called will be easier if you start with realistic expectations. When you think about it, what we want is not only that our dogs come when called, but also that they not run away in the first place. What fun would it be to have a dog who always comes when he is called, but as soon as you let him go, he takes off, and you have to call him again? Everyone wants a dog who sticks around or stays in the yard without having to be constantly called. As it turns out, the easiest dog to train to come is the dog who never wants to leave in the first place, and the hardest one to train is the one who is obsessed with getting away.

Some dogs are easier to train than others. Some dogs will never be safe off leash, and others you couldn't lose if you tried. Knowing what factors affect this will help you to understand your dog and to have realistic expectations regarding his training. Such expectations will help prevent you from feeling angry and frustrated. These emotions interfere with good training by affecting your judgment and your relationship with your dog.

A major factor that determines the ease of training your dog to come when called is the age that training is started. The earlier you start, the more you can prevent bad habits from forming. As we have already discussed, puppies have a natural instinct to stay close to their owners and come when called. Starting training early takes advantage of this. With any early start, you can avoid becoming dependent on the leash to get your dog's attention.

Owners who do not start training early get into a vicious cycle. They do not let their dog off leash because he doesn't come when called, so the dog becomes frustrated from lack of exercise and freedom. The frustration builds, so the next time he gets free he will run farther and longer, and the owner is more convinced than ever to never let his dog off leash.

A second factor in training your dog to come when called is your dog's personality, which is partially related to his breed, or mixture of breeds. Of course, not all dogs within a breed are the same, but looking at what the breed was historically bred to do will give you a clue to the ease with which your dog can be trained to come. As a *general rule*, dogs bred to work independently of man and to have a high energy level are harder to train to come when called. Northern breeds, like the Siberian Husky,

The joy of off-leash freedom. (Irish Setter)

Playing Frisbee is good off-leash exercise. (Irish Setter)

are difficult because they were bred to run long distances and have independent personalities. Chow Chows are independent and assertive, but fortunately have a lower energy level than Siberians. Sighthounds, which are dogs bred to instinctively chase things that move, love to run and are easily distracted by any moving thing they see. Sighthounds include breeds such as Greyhounds, Afghans, Salukis, Borzois, and Whippets. Doberman Pinschers seem a lot like sighthounds—easily distracted and full of energy. Terriers can be difficult because they are independent and energetic.

Some of the hunting breeds, such as Setters and Pointers, are also hard to train to come because of their innate desire to hunt and their high energy levels. The breeds bred to herd, such as German Shepherds, Border Collies, or Shetland Sheepdogs, are usually the easiest to train because they have little desire to leave in the first place. In between are the rest of the breeds.

The individual personality of your dog will also affect his willingness to come when called. An independent dog is much harder to train than a dependent one, and a bold dog will be more difficult than a shy dog. Females are generally easier to train to come than are males who have not been castrated. Such males are distracted by their hormonally influenced drives. Some dogs have a stronger chase instinct than others and are more likely to run off after a squirrel. A dog doesn't have to be of a hunting breed to like to hunt.

A third factor is the environment in which your dog lives. It is difficult to train a dog to come if he lives in a neighborhood where the houses are

A dog who doesn't come when called is not only frustrating, but can be in danger of being hit by a car. (Tibetan Terrier)

close together and the yards are not fenced. The distractions of people, children, cats, and other dogs are too great for most dogs to resist.

I have two friends who have dogs who always come when called, and these dogs are good examples of how these factors work. One is a German Shepherd, and the other is a Golden Retriever. The German Shepherd, Raven, is the kind of dog you couldn't lose if you tried. Her owner and I often go for walks in the woods with our dogs. Her dog comes better than mine do, even though Raven's training consists of just one basic obedience class many years ago and mine have AKC obedience titles and years of training. Her dog is very dependent and just doesn't want to leave her. It is unusual for Raven to get more than 25 feet from her owner, and she used to go only a few feet until my dogs encouraged her to go farther. If we come across a squirrel on our walks, my dogs are off and running, but Raven never chases it at all. She has no urge to chase animals. Raven is also a little shy and not attracted to other people, so she doesn't run off to greet neighbors or hikers we meet on the trail. Raven gets long, off-leash walks almost every day, so she gets plenty of exercise, and has since she was a puppy. At home, Raven has a fenced backyard, so there is no problem there.

The Golden Retriever is named Zandy. Zandy lives on property consisting of several acres at the end of a lane quite a distance from the main road. Zandy's owners began taking lessons from me when Zandy was 10 weeks old. She has another dog, a cat, two horses, and two children to keep her company and to play with. Her owner does not work and is home all day. Zandy stays in or out as she pleases, and can be trusted to remain around the house without direct supervision. She is an easygoing dog of medium energy level. She is not an adventurous dog and prefers being a follower.

These dogs have several things in common. They are both females of breeds that are generally easy to train to come when called. Both get a lot of off-leash exercise that started when they were young puppies. Neither has a strong urge to hunt. They both have dependent personalities and are not bold. Neither is a high-energy dog. In both cases, the fact that they come when called is dependent on factors other than training alone. It is also interesting to note that both are natural retrievers. Natural retrieving instincts seem to be associated with trainability and a willingness on the dog's part to follow his owner's directions.

Before you get too discouraged because your dog isn't the right breed, doesn't have the right personality, and doesn't live in the best situation, let

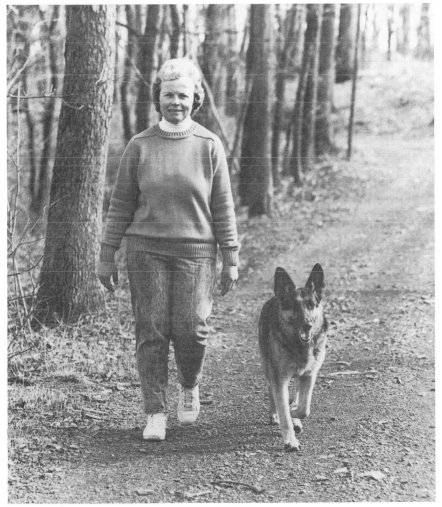

Nancy and Raven.

me assure you that you can improve your dog's off-leash responsiveness through good training. But you must have realistic expectations. I have been able to exercise all my dogs off leash, even though they include an Irish Setter, a Borzoi, and a Greyhound—breeds not known for their off-leash obedience. I walk my dogs off leash every day, so coming when called is daily work for me and my dogs. In spite of all of their training, if they are chasing a squirrel, I cannot call them and make them stop. However, I can turn my Greyhound loose in an open field and admire her speed and grace as she runs. My husband and I can play Frisbee with them and take them swimming. Teaching a dog to come when called is hard work, but the rewards are great.

The Foundation

If you turned to this chapter first before reading the rest of the book because coming when called is a major problem with your dog, you are going to have to go back and read at least the previous chapter. You will do better if you read everything except the housebreaking chapter. The training discussed in this chapter is based on what you have taught your dog from the material presented in the previous chapter. You shouldn't expect your dog to come when he is 50 feet away from you if he doesn't understand what the command means in the first place or if he doesn't respond reliably to it when he is 5 feet away and on a leash. Make sure your dog will pay attention to you and respond promptly to all the basic commands on leash in the places where you would like him to come when called. The bonding created by the basic training will greatly improve your dog's responsiveness to you in general, which in turn makes it easier to train him to come when called.

Don't make the mistake of skipping the basic training in chapter 5 because you think that your dog already knows what "come" means. If you haven't made a specific effort to teach him what "come" means, he doesn't. This is a common error because dogs do respond when you call them some of the time, even though they don't know what the word "come" means. In young puppies, it is a natural response for them to come toward you when they hear your voice. A dog may know his name and come sometimes when he hears it, but that is not the same as knowing that "come" means to move close enough to you so you could touch him.

Unintentional Punishment: Training Your Dog Not to Come

Many people unintentionally train their dogs *not* to come. There are many ways to do this, and you want to identify and avoid all of them.

It should be obvious to anyone that calling a dog to you and then punishing him will discourage the dog from coming in the future. If someone called you to them, then slapped you when you got there, would you want to come the next time they called you? While the answer seems obvious, it is hard to control the urge to do just that when you come upon some "evidence of crime" in your house, such as a pillow torn to shreds or a warm puddle. Resist the urge or you will be training your dog not to come. This is the kind of situation we discussed in the first chapter, where anger can overcome reason and add up to bad training.

The situation in which anger is most likely to cause trouble is when your dog runs away. For some reason, probably because you are being more careless, this always seems to happen when you are in a hurry. Instead of being on time for your appointment, you find yourself chasing your dog through the neighborhood for half an hour. You keep calling your dog, and he finally comes to you. That's when anger overcomes reason, and you start to punish him by hitting him, shaking him by his collar, or yelling at him. What have you really done? You've punished him for coming. This makes it less likely, not more likely, that your dog will come in the future. Nonetheless, some people persist in punishing their dogs in this situation, usually increasing the punishment with each occurrence, even though it is not working. Taken to extremes, this creates a dog who runs away and then *will not* come home out of fear of punishment.

What should you do if you find yourself in this situation? Chalk it up to experience, promise yourself to never let it happen again, grit your teeth, and praise your dog for coming. Okay, you don't have to be enthusiastic. But you have to make sure your dog knows it is safe to come to you should it happen again.

Most situations of unintentional punishment are more subtle. Punishing your dog for coming can be something as simple as just always calling your dog when you want him to come inside. While this may not seem like punishment, if your dog associates being called with his playtime being ended, he is unlikely to want to come. Or perhaps you call him to lock him in his crate before you go to work. Avoid calling your dog for anything he finds unpleasant, such as cutting his toenails or giving him a bath.

Of course, you have to somehow get your dog to come inside, or into his crate, or into the bathtub. There are two solutions to this dilemma. The first is to call him to you, preferably some distance from the back door, the crate, or the bathroom (the final destination), reward him, spend a few minutes petting him, and then lead him by the collar to where you want him.

The second method is to teach your dog a separate command that means to go inside. That way, your command to come is kept separate from any bad associations and is ready when you need it for emergencies. That's what I do. The command I use is "inside!" For the crate, I use "get in your crate." These commands I can back up with force if my dogs don't obey, and this will not destroy their pleasant associations with the word "come." I use "inside" for coming into the house and for getting into the car. My dogs seem more willing to obey the inside command than the come command in those situations. It almost seems as if they were confused when I called them to come when they knew that what I really wanted was for them to go inside. Of course, when they come into the house or get in their crates, they often receive a reward.

A variation of training a dog not to come is teaching him to play keep-away. We discussed this in chapter 5, when you learned how to teach your dog to come, sit, and let you touch his collar. However, it bears repeating: Don't lunge and grab your dog, and don't chase him when you call him.

The Long Line: A Life Saver

The long line is an important tool in teaching your dog to come when called. It gives your dog a sense of freedom while you maintain control and keep him safe.

The long line is simply a 30- to 40-foot leash. It is also called a check cord. It can be made of many different materials and can either be purchased ready-made or made by you. Cotton or nylon webbing, any kind of rope, or nylon cord can be used along with a well-fitting buckle collar that will not slip over your dog's head if your dog pulls on it. A dog who charges to the end of a 40-foot rope and is wearing a choke collar may damage his neck when he hits the end of it.

I like polypropylene rope of about three-eighths-inch width because it is strong enough for a medium- to large-size dog but it is not overly heavy and it doesn't tangle easily. It also doesn't soak up moisture like cotton webbing does. You can just buy 30 to 40 feet of rope in a hardware store and a medium-size bolt snap to tie onto the end of it. Make sure the bolt snap is no larger than necessary to hold your dog. Getting an enormous, heavy bolt snap that would hold an elephant and acts as an anchor for your dog to drag around defeats the purpose of the long line. You want the dog to have a sense of freedom, and this would be negated by dragging around a heavy rope with a big bolt snap. If you have a small dog, you will have to use a light-weight cord and a very small bolt snap. For small dogs, I use parachute cord that I purchase at an army surplus store. Unfortunately, it tangles easily.

When to Use the Long Line

The long line is used after you have taught your dog the meaning of the word "come," off leash, in a confined area, and you are ready to move to a place where your dog may not come. Start in a place with a minimum of distractions.

Just because your dog zooms to you whenever you call him in the house, do not assume that he knows what you mean when you call him outside. When the situation changes by your moving from a familiar situation, such as inside the house or in a fenced backyard, to a new place, your dog may not understand what you want. He only associates the command with a particular place, and it may take him a while to learn what the "come" command means in a new place and situation. Be patient, and don't be frustrated by this temporary relapse.

The long line is a good tool to use when a puppy outgrows the stage where he naturally sticks close to his owner. You will know when it is time. It usually happens between the ages of 12 and 16 weeks. Your puppy looks up when you call, and turns and heads in the opposite direction. If you have done a lot of early puppy training, this stage may be delayed until a later age. When this happens, do not yell, scream, and chase after your puppy. Calmly walk toward him and keep walking after him until you can call him to you and take hold of his collar. If he is heading in a dangerous direction, loudly call his name and run in the opposite direction, encouraging him to chase you. Then do not let him off the long line for the next two to four weeks.

Not every dog needs to be trained on a long line. With the right dog in the right environment and the proper early puppy training, you may be able to skip it.

How to Use the Long Line

The most important rule in using the long line is to avoid keeping constant tension on it. Your dog should not pull you around on it, and neither should you pull your dog. Keeping tension on the line destroys the feeling of freedom you are trying to give your dog. It is best if you do not hold on to the line at all, but let your dog drag it. If, however, you think your dog will bolt and run even with the long line on, hang on to the end of it. If you have to do this, wear gloves to prevent rope burns.

Don't forget to have a pocketful of treats when you take your dog out on the long line. Wait until his back is turned to you, or he is distracted by sniffing at something. Call his name to get his attention, and then give him the command "come!" Remember to give him consistent commands, using the exact same words and *same tone of voice* you used when teaching him to come and sit for food. Make your commands sound inviting, not like a drill sergeant's order.

If your dog turns toward you when he hears his name and starts toward you, praise him like crazy all the way in and drop down to your knees to receive him with open arms. Be super-enthusiastic with your praise, and give him a treat. Sometimes it is good to dispense with the formality of the sit and just let him plow into you.

If your dog does not turn toward you when he hears his name and the come command, give him a sharp tug on the line. Do not use the line to drag him in like a fish on a line. Keep giving him sharp tugs on the line and encouraging him with your voice until he starts coming on his own. When he gets there, even though he needed help, praise him and give him a treat.

Most likely at this stage of the game he doesn't understand what you want, so you must help him understand by rewarding him when he gets to you.

After your dog receives his praise and treat, it is very important that you then release him with an "okay" command and allow him to move around freely again. You want your dog to think that "come" means "time to take a break and get a treat," not "this is the end of playtime." Remember, don't unintentionally punish your dog for coming by always using the command to end your dog's playtime.

Once your dog is responding well on the long line, so well that you don't feel you need to hold on to the line, it is time to make the training more challenging by adding distractions. Take him out on the long line while the neighborhood gang of six-year-olds is running around screaming, and call him away if he tries to join in. Leave a piece of bread lying in the yard. Casually approach the area where the bread is until your dog is sniffing or

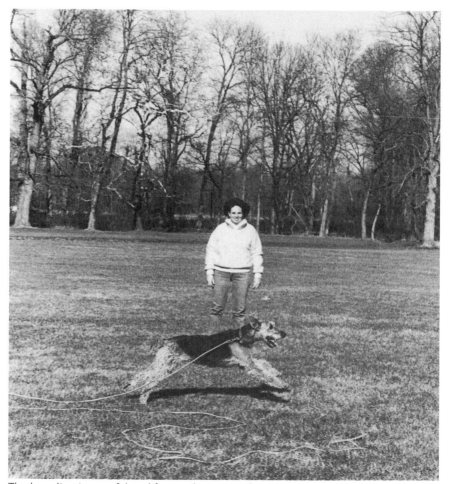

The long line is a useful tool for teaching your dog to come. (Airedale)

eating it. Then call him. Again, give him a good tug on the line if he doesn't start toward you. It is okay if he brings the piece of bread with him when he comes, just as long as he comes.

If you walk your dog in a park and let him play with other dogs, let him play with the long line on, then occasionally call him to you for a treat. Be careful not to jerk the line if any of the other dogs are tangled up in it.

As mentioned earlier, teaching a dog to come when called also involves teaching him how far he can go from you by calling him when he gets too far away. Walk him around the perimeter of your yard and correct him if he steps over the line. Remember to keep the line slack; don't tighten up on the line as he approaches the boundary of your yard and prevent him from leaving. Let him step over the line, then say, "No, come!" If he does, praise him profusely. If he doesn't, give him a jerk on the line. Keep repeating this until the lesson is learned.

For some dogs, this may be as far as they progress. They may always have to be on a long line for their own safety. Some may be safe to take off leash in some places and not in others. For instance, many dogs may be fine off leash in a big, open field while you are keeping them busy with a game of Frisbee, but they cannot be trusted in their own unfenced backyards with the distractions of other dogs and people and the danger of a street close by. A good compromise, if you don't have a fenced yard, may be to take your dog to another place several times a week for off-leash exercise.

The Off-Leash Dog

Hopefully, your long line work will progress until you are ready to try some off-leash work. You should first be comfortable with giving your dog a lot of freedom on the long line. You may want to gradually reduce your and your dog's dependence on the long line by reducing its weight and its length, until your dog is dragging a three-foot piece of lightweight cord.

Your chances of being successful when you take your dog off leash can be increased by setting up the situation to your advantage. Choose the best place and the best time. First of all, dogs always come better when called in unfamiliar places. Some suggestions for testing your dog's training are a friend's fenced backyard or a tennis court that is entirely fenced. If you are starting in an unfenced area, make sure you are far from a road. Watch out for wildlife that your dog might chase. I prefer to use a trail in a wooded area rather than a big, open field. The disadvantage of an open field is that a dog can see farther than in the woods and may chase something he sees quite a distance away. Dogs can detect movement farther away than people can. Also, your dog can get quite a distance from you yet still have the security of being able to see you. The turns in a wooded trail help prevent a dog from getting too far ahead because he won't be able to see you.

The best time to try your dog off leash is in warmer weather. The heat will decrease his endurance. It helps if your dog has already been thoroughly exercised *before* you take the leash off. An hour's worth of jogging would be best, but if that's not possible, try a long walk in the area where you intend to let him off leash.

Increase your dog's motivation by bringing special food treats with you and making sure he is hungry. Don't use your everyday training treats. How would your dog feel about slices of pepperoni? I'll never forget what one student brought for her dog's first time off leash. The dog was a Borzoi who had been kept on a chain in the backyard most of his life. He and his owner had successfully completed a basic obedience class. When she showed up at the place at which we had decided to meet, she got out of the car with an *entire roasted chicken* wrapped in aluminum foil!

It helps to have dogs along who are very good about coming when called and don't like getting far from their owners. Having other dogs to play with will motivate your dog to stay with the group.

The first time Shannon, an adult Golden Retriever/Irish Setter mix, was taken off leash is a good example of setting up the situation for success. Shannon lives with her owner at a horse stable. Unfortunately, even though Shannon lived on several acres, whenever she got loose outside, she ran across the road. When her owner finally caught her after a long chase, he punished her. This resulted in Shannon staying away longer and longer, and becoming harder and harder to catch. It also resulted in Shannon's gaining a tremendous amount of weight from lack of exercise.

After some basic training, we were ready to try Shannon off leash. We started out by jogging her on leash about a mile on a warm day. Because Shannon had received little exercise lately, she was in poor shape and got tired easily. Then we walked Shannon to the far end of the stable property along with two dogs who were friendly with other dogs and pretty good about coming when called. Shannon's owner filled his pockets with slices of hot dogs and made sure Shannon knew they were there. Then we turned Shannon loose and started walking. It is much easier to keep a dog with you if you are walking somewhere than if you are just standing still. If you are walking, your dog is occupied with keeping up with you and cannot get too distracted—but if you stand still, many dogs will gradually drift away and become involved in pursuing their own interests.

Shannon did fine. Her owner called her back every couple of minutes, gave her a slice of hot dog, and released her to continue playing. The hardest part was keeping her owner from panicking every time Shannon got more than a few feet away. When we walked back and got close to the road, we called Shannon in and put her on leash. Shannon cannot be turned loose at the stable without supervision, as their previous dog could, but at least she can get some exercise off leash.

Once you have been successful in letting your dog off leash, you have broken the cycle of your dog running away because of lack of exercise and freedom. Prevent the cycle from starting again by keeping him exercised. It is helpful to occasionally let your dog run until he is tired, instead of stopping when *you* want to quit. You can gradually give him more freedom in more challenging situations.

Keeping Up Your Come Training

Training your dog to come never really ends. As with anything you teach your dog, any behaviors that are not reinforced, by either reward or punishment, will gradually disappear, and that includes coming when called. However, unlike losing your dog's training to not pull on the leash, losing your come training may cost your dog his life.

The first rule is not to wait until your dog stops coming when called to do something about it. Maintain your come training. Always reward your dog for coming when you call him. Praise him enthusiastically every single time. Never take his coming for granted. Every once in a while, give him a food reward. Try not to call him more than four times without giving him a reward.

You need to know what to do if your dog doesn't come when you call him when he is off leash *after* he has been trained. First of all, don't keep calling him, repeating the command. This will just teach him to ignore you. You will be untraining your dog by calling him repeatedly and allowing him to ignore your commands. And don't chase after him, unless it is an emergency. Don't change your tone of voice. If you sound angry or scared, he will be less likely to come to you. He may not even recognize the command if your tone of voice is different.

There are times you can punish your dog if he does not come and improve his response. This must be done the right way and at the right time to be effective. You must not do this until you are absolutely sure that your dog understands what "come" means. He must have been responding to the command most of the time in a majority of situations before you attempt to punish him when he does not come.

If your dog is sniffing around and ignoring you, just walk up to him quietly. I find that if I am ready to explode with anger, I can sometimes cover it up by humming quietly as I approach. Then, once I get my hands on my dog, I repeat the "come" command so my dog knows why he is being disciplined and give him a good shake or jerk on the collar.

Sometimes things aren't that easy. I remember the first time my Greyhound puppy ignored my "inside" command. It was a lovely day, and she just didn't want to stop playing. I was in an irritated mood. She took one look at me, knew what mood I was in, and became determined not to be caught, with all the defiance a five-month-old puppy could muster. Now,

A tattoo provides your dog with permanent identification and is good insurance against theft or loss.

how much chance do you think I had of catching a dog bred to sprint at 40 miles an hour? I took a deep breath, tried to tell myself it was a wonderful training opportunity even though it was going to make me late and disrupt my entire day, accepted the fact that I couldn't change it anyway, and started humming as I walked after her. We went in circles around the house for 45 minutes. I didn't want to call her to me at this point because if she came to me, I would have to praise her. She finally stopped, and I could walk up to her and take hold of her collar. At that point I repeated the "inside" command, gave her a very hard shake, and abruptly marched her into the house. I was very dramatic in order to impress her. I never again had trouble getting her to come inside.

Watch for little signs that the training is fading. The first sign is usually that your dog stops coming on the first command, but waits until you have called him several times. Then you find yourself getting louder. If you find your dog frequently ignoring your command to come, and a few corrections don't work, go back to the long line for a refresher course. Don't be lazy; go after your dog and get him when he doesn't come.

Fenced yards can be an enemy of training a dog to come because you don't often need to call your dog if he is always in a fenced yard or in the house. Your dog won't get much practice. Be careful to keep up the training.

Remember that anytime you take your dog off leash you are taking a chance. Make sure your dog is well identified in case he is separated from you. An identification tag is a must, but sometimes dogs escape without it. There are two alternatives for providing permanent identification of your dog. One is a tattoo, which is a number that is inscribed inside your dog's thigh. This can be uncomfortable for the few minutes it takes, but it can be done without anesthesia. A good time to have your dog tattooed is when your dog is being neutered or spayed. This number should be registered with a national registry, such as AKC's Companion Animal Recovery program.

Another way to permanently identify your dog is with a microchip. A microchip is a tiny transponder the size of a grain of rice that is imbedded under your dog's skin in his shoulder area. It can be read by a handheld scanner. In a process like giving a vaccination, chips are implanted by veterinarians or other trained people. This number can be registered with the AKC. I recommend having both a tattoo and a microchip.

In spite of all the training, there is always a possibility of your dog running into the street and being hit by a car. I know my dogs get more minor injuries, such as cuts and sprains, because they are allowed the freedom to play off leash. Balancing concern for your dog's safety with concern for the quality of his life is a difficult decision to make.

A tired dog gets into less trouble (if you don't count sleeping on the furniture!)
(Greyhound)

7

Exercise: The Magic Problem Solver

The members of the genus *canis*, which includes wolves, coyotes, jackals, and domestic dogs, are predators that hunt by traveling long distances looking for prey and then chasing them. Wolves, a close wild relative of dogs, can travel an average of 15 miles a day. Dogs, except for those breeds that have been radically changed by man's selective breeding, have the endurance and energy of their wild ancestors. Problems arise when this energy is not given an outlet.

Dogs who do not get enough exercise become frustrated. This frustration often causes undesirable behaviors: chewing, barking, digging, running away, and general unruliness, to name a few. Almost any behavior problem can be improved by providing a dog with more exercise. A tired dog doesn't need to find an outlet for his energy. He is less likely to get into trouble. A tired dog is a well-behaved dog.

All the training in the world is not a substitute for adequate exercise. Even though training can tire a dog, it cannot relax a dog the way exercise can. Training and exercise depend on each other. It is hard to exercise a dog who pulls on the leash and won't come when called. On the other hand, it is hard to train a dog who hasn't had enough exercise.

Providing a dog with adequate exercise is not easy. You come home from a hard day at work, ready to collapse, only to be faced with a dog who has been sleeping all day and is now bursting with energy. However, this is a sacrifice you should be prepared to make if you own a dog. If you can see it as a time for you to relax, too, it won't seem like so much of a chore.

How Much?

The amount of exercise a dog needs is different for every dog and depends on various factors. Some of these factors were discussed in chapter 4. Obviously, a dog with a high energy level needs more exercise. Your dog's breed will have an effect on his need for exercise. Among those breeds developed for tireless activity are sled dogs, hunting dogs, and herding dogs. An older dog needs less exercise than a younger dog. Another factor is whether your dog is an only dog or has another dog to encourage him to play and exercise.

A dog's exercise needs do *not* depend on his size. Small dogs do not necessarily need less exercise than large dogs. Some large dogs, especially some of the giant breeds, are very phlegmatic, while a small terrier can be like a missile on four legs. A Mastiff may only need a leisurely stroll around the block, while a Parson Russell Terrier may be going strong after two miles of brisk walking.

Like humans, dogs derive the most health and mental benefits from exercise if it is extended aerobic exercise, not just a fast sprint. Don't make the mistake of thinking that because your dog is panting, he is tired and should stop exercising. Dogs pant to cool themselves, much like we sweat. It does not mean they are gasping for oxygen.

Access to a fenced yard is not enough to provide most dogs with adequate exercise. They won't exercise on their own, other than perhaps a fast dash around the yard with the initial burst of energy. Left alone in a yard for long periods, they become bored and can develop behavior problems, such as digging or excessive barking. Tying a dog out or using an overhead trolley certainly does not constitute exercise.

Exercise must be limited for dogs with physical problems, puppies, and old dogs. Puppies need short, frequent bursts of exercise, and should never be forced to exercise longer than they wish. As dogs get older they need less exercise. Old dogs derive many health benefits from regular exercise, even if they don't need it from a behavioral viewpoint. A brisk walk of a mile may be just the thing for a 10-year-old dog, even if he has arthritis and reduced heart function. Exercise encourages regular bowel movements, keeps up muscle tone, preserves range of motion in the joints, and provides much-needed mental stimulation. When deciding about cutting back on an older dog's exercise, keep in mind that dogs age at different rates, with large dogs having shorter life spans and showing signs of age earlier than small dogs.

Whenever you are exercising your dog, you must be careful about the heat. Dogs do not cool as efficiently as humans do because they cannot sweat through their skin. As mentioned above, a dog cools himself by panting, which circulates blood through the lungs and nose where it comes into contact with cooler surfaces. When you are hot, your dog is hotter. An overheated dog can die of heatstroke.

So what is a good amount of exercise for your dog? Let his behavior tell you. Is he relaxed or restless? Think about any behavior problems your dog may have. Is the cause lack of training, or is it lack of exercise? Most likely, it is a combination of both. However, if inadequate exercise is part of the cause, training alone will not solve your problem. The answer is giving your dog more exercise.

Walking Your Dog: Good for Both of You

The classic way to exercise your dog is walking him on leash. If this is the way you are going to exercise your dog, make sure exercising is what you are doing and not just giving him a chance to relieve himself on the neighbors' lawns. Walk briskly and do not allow him to stop. He should relieve himself at home before you leave. *Do not let him stop to sniff.* You both have to keep moving to get good exercise.

Train your dog to walk without pulling, and then never allow him to pull again when you are walking him. It is not good for your dog to be dragging you down the street, gasping and wheezing for air. And it is not good for your arm! You will have to be stubborn because it is not natural for an excited dog to walk at a slow enough pace to match yours. Make sure that anyone who walks him insists on him not pulling; consistency is important if walking without pulling is going to become a habit. If you walk your dog in an open area, you may want to try walking him on a retractable leash. It will give him a little more freedom, and he won't pull as much.

Greyhounds used for coursing rabbits in England were walked 5 to 10 miles a day. Now that's a walk! You may not want to do as much, but remember that extended exercise is best for your dog. This means at least 20 minutes of walking for a little dog, and more for a larger dog. Two miles would be good for medium and large dogs.

Do you have a dog who is very friendly with other dogs? You're lucky. However, even though your dog is friendly, many dogs are not. Some are very frightened of other dogs. Please respect them. I had a dog who was aggressive if other dogs charged up to him, even if to be friendly. I hated when owners yelled, "It's okay. My dog is friendly," as their dogs dragged them to my poor dog. Then, when my dog complained about the obnoxious greeting, the other owners thought my dog was at fault. Don't be a rude dog owner.

A wonderful aspect of walking your dog on leash, even if it isn't as efficient as exercising a dog off leash, is that it often gives you an opportunity to meet people. You may even meet someone with whom you can form a dog play group!

Finding a Place to Exercise Off Leash

Off-leash exercise is the most relaxing kind of exercise for a dog. Free from restraint, a dog can really be a dog. You can enjoy the beauty and expression of their movements. However, finding a place you can safely and legally do this is difficult.

Finding a good place often requires some detective work. Ask other dog owners where they exercise their dogs. A farmer might give you permission to use his fields when the crops aren't growing. If you have a friend who is a realtor, he may be able to tell you where there is vacant land for sale that you can use until it is sold.

Trails where you and your dog can walk together are good for off-leash exercise. Keeping your dog with you when he is off leash is easier if you are going somewhere, not just standing still. Walking also encourages your dog to exercise more. People who like to hike may also be able to give you some tips, as may books on local hiking trails. Look for side trails off the more popular trails where you can avoid bothering other people. Buy a topographic map and peruse it for old logging trails. Check out state game lands and snowmobile trails. Ask hunters, especially those who hunt with dogs, for suggestions. Be careful if you are using areas where people hunt; know when the various hunting seasons start and end so you can avoid being out during those times.

While parks are more convenient for exercising than the alternatives mentioned above, they must be used with great care and caution. It is almost always against the law or rules of the park to let your dog off leash. You will

Dog parks are a great way to exercise and socialize your dog.

be able to do so only if you are very careful to avoid infringing on the rights of other park users. Any time you have your dog off leash, it is of paramount importance that you respect the rights of non-dog owners. Previous failure to do so on the part of many dog owners has resulted in greater and greater restrictions on the places our dogs can go. Your dog has to be very responsive to your commands, never wandering far from you and always coming when called. In a park, other people and dogs present a strong distraction that makes control of your dog difficult. Visiting a park during off hours, either early in the morning or at dusk, is a good idea. Popular additions to parks now are dog parks, which are fenced areas set aside for use of dog owners. And popular they are! A dog park that recently opened in my area was swamped with people, some of whom drove a long distance. Dogs parks can be private or public. There is sometimes an entrance fee. Please read the section below on dog play groups for information on dogs interacting. A dog park works best when there is a separate area for small dogs. Interactions at dog parks can build confidence and be great socialization, but be careful that your dog isn't bullied. If your dog is frightened, he may become aggressive. If there are no good places in your area to allow your dog to run off leash, try to get your local government to open a dog park. It's a great way to keep the peace between dog and non-dog people.

You must also respect the rights of dog owners who keep their dogs on leash and may not want other dogs near them. As the owner of a dog who is sometimes aggressive with other dogs, I know it is infuriating to have to lift Sabre off his front feet by means of his collar and let him strangle while another dog who is off leash runs around him, ignoring his owner's commands to come and eluding all attempts at capture.

Hopefully, it is not necessary to remind you that you must clean up after your dog. My favorite cleanup method is a plastic bag pulled over my hand like a glove. Once the stool is picked up, I pull the plastic bag back over my hand and knot it. These bags are convenient to carry in your pocket. Use a part of the park that is least used, away from eating areas and places where children play. Don't ruin a privilege for everyone; *clean up after your dog.* Keep in mind that even if you clean up after your dog, there is some residue left in the grass that picnickers shouldn't have to sit in or children play in.

If you are going to exercise your dog off leash, there is always a risk that he will become separated from you and lost, so good identification is necessary. The best form of identification is a tattoo, which was described in the previous chapter. Even if your dog is not exercised off leash, a tattoo is still a good idea. It is insurance against your dog being stolen. Dog theft is a multi-million-dollar business in this country. Stolen dogs are sold to dealers, who in turn sell them to laboratories. Since laboratories do not buy tattooed dogs, such dogs aren't stolen; if they are, they are turned loose. Tattooing is not expensive, and is the best insurance that, if you ever lose your dog, he will be returned.

Even if it means driving a half hour to get there, or spending a lot of time training your dog to come when called, you and your dog will both be happier if he can get some off-leash exercise.

Dog Play Groups

On the first night of my puppy training classes, I tell all the owners to take the leashes off their puppies and let them play. At first no one wants to do it. They are afraid there will be fights or a puppy will be hurt. After a lot of persuasion—and often I unsnap the leashes myself—the puppies are turned loose and start to play. And the owners start to smile. It is fun to watch the puppies run and wrestle and tumble around the room, having the time of their lives. Some of the puppies may be a little shy at first, but they join in eventually.

After a few minutes of playtime, we begin class with puppies who are more able to concentrate because they aren't bursting with energy. After class, the puppies are rewarded with another play session. The owners are rewarded with tired puppies who go home and collapse. I also try to have a playtime after the beginners class for dogs over five months old. Because the dogs are older, not all of them will want to play. There may be two uncastrated males who are likely to fight if given the opportunity. Or there may be a dog who has lacked socialization with other dogs to the extent that he cannot interact normally with other dogs. After these dogs leave, the rest of the dogs are allowed to play.

You can also exercise your dog this way and provide him with the opportunity to socialize with members of his own species by forming a dog play

These two Belgian Tervurens may look like they are fighting, but they are really playing.

group. This is a group of dogs who gets together to play on a regular but informal basis. It is especially beneficial for a dog who doesn't live with another dog. You can start by just getting together with one other dog and owner, and add more as interest develops. Whether the group meets every morning or only once a week or month, any opportunity for your dog to play is better than none.

The advantage of a regular play group is that your dog will play better with dogs he knows well. As the dogs become better friends, they will become less inhibited with each other in their interactions. They will get to know what games the other dogs like to play and what behavior they will or will not tolerate. The dogs will develop their own special games, complete with elaborate rules that escape a human's understanding. They will even develop special friendships. A regular play group is especially helpful if your dog tends to be uncomfortable or even aggressive around dogs he doesn't know.

The dogs will get along better if they are off leash. A leash prevents dogs from being able to communicate normally because it restricts their body language. Dogs also are more likely to fight if they are on leash. In fact, a dog who behaves aggressively toward other dogs when he is on leash may be fine with other dogs when he is off leash. If a dog has to be on leash, it is best to use a long line.

A dog play group is a good way to provide your dog with exercise.

Dog play groups can meet in a variety of places. It is best if you select a site where the dogs can be off leash. Public places should be avoided except during off-hours. A pack of dogs playing together can be very frightening to some people. Sometimes the dog owners in a development can meet in an empty lot at the end of the development. A dog owner without a fenced yard may be grateful for an opportunity to let his dog off leash in someone's fenced yard. Tennis courts may be good when they are not being used. And you don't have to stand still while the dogs are playing. One of the things I enjoy most in life is to go for a hike in the woods with a group of friends and their dogs. It is not unusual for us to have 6 to 8 dogs along, and we once had 16!

Dog play groups can be combined with dog training. Besides providing you with an opportunity to train your dog around the distractions of other dogs, you can get advice from the other owners. It is more fun to train as part of a group than by yourself. Don't forget to line all the dogs up on a sit-stay and take a picture of your dog with his buddies.

It is likely that when dogs play together there may be a fight. They are usually not serious, although they may sound horrible. Dogs rarely hurt each other in a fight, if neither dog has a severe psychological problem and if they have enough space to separate. If one occurs, do not scream and get hysterical. That will only make the fight worse. Wait a few seconds and see if it will resolve itself without your interference. Then try yelling loudly in a firm tone of voice and telling them to stop. If this doesn't work, separate them by grabbing their tails and pulling. You can also grab the skin and fur on the back of the dogs' necks to separate them. Do not reach in and try to grab for collars. That is a good way to get your hand in the way of their mouths and get bitten.

When you become more skilled at reading dog body language, you will be able to see the fights developing and warn the dogs to behave before the fight happens. This requires a dog who is very responsive to commands, however. Typically in our play group, the male dogs will start stalking each other. We just warn them with "Boooys . . ." and because the dogs are trained, they separate and find something else to do.

Don't mistake rough play for fighting. There can be a lot of growling and biting between good friends. A student of mine says people have come to her door to warn her that her dogs were killing each other in her backyard when they were only playing. It amazes me to watch my two dogs, Zephyr and Sabre, chew on each other. Zephyr has the typical, tissue-paper-thin, fragile skin of a Greyhound that seems to split open incredibly easily. However, Sabre has never broken her skin in even their roughest wrestling matches.

Avoid giving the dogs toys if they might fight over them. However, sometimes an old rag can stimulate a good game of tug-of-war or catch-me-if-you-can. Dogs who won't chase a ball normally may do so when there is another dog to compete with.

Watching dogs play is entertaining and relaxing. It is fascinating to observe their behavior with each other and how they communicate. You can learn a lot about dog body language. And you will probably spend more time exercising your dog if you have company. Everybody benefits from a dog play group!

Jogging with Your Dog

I was surprised the other day to talk to someone who thought it was cruel to make a dog jog with you. She ought to be at my house when my husband starts to get dressed to go jogging. The canine jogging addicts I live with go crazy. They spin through the house like whirling dervishes, whining in anticipation, both hoping to be the first to go. Age having its privileges, it is the custom in our house for the oldest dog to go first. So Sabre lunges out the door, biting at the leash in his anxiety to get started.

Good heeling is a must for jogging, and it can be a challenge to teach a dog not to get excited and pull when you are running. Your dog has to understand that he cannot lunge after squirrels that cross your path or fight with dogs who might chase you. A prong collar often provides a good solution. Be careful if you are using a buckle collar that your dog cannot pull back out of it if he is startled. Since you are more visible than your dog, you will want to jog so that you are the one closest to the traffic. This means that if your dog is used to heeling on the left, you will have to jog facing traffic.

Not all dogs like or should be jogging. A puppy should be at least eight months old before you begin, and older if he is a large, heavy-boned dog. Jogging is obviously not suitable for very small dogs. Dogs with hip dysplasia should jog only if a veterinarian has first been consulted. It may be that jogging moderate distances may build muscles that would help a dysplastic dog. If you have a breed prone to hip dysplasia, which includes most large breeds, avoid jogging if there is any sign of a limp or even a problem keeping up with you. Again, consult a veterinarian to be sure. Never force a dog to jog.

How far you run with your dog is determined by your dog's and your condition. Two miles is probably a good distance, but even one mile of jogging can have a big effect on your dog's behavior. The maximum distance my husband has ever run with our dogs is 6.2 miles, the distance of a 10-kilometer race, which they sometimes do together. A dog must be over 1 year of age to do this kind of distance, and we advocate reducing the distance as the dog gets over 8 years old. Elderly dog jogging addicts can be a problem, as it is hard to explain to them that they are too old to continue jogging. We deal with the problem by taking our senior citizens over 10 years old on "pretend jogs." These are slow jogs of one-quarter to one-half mile to pacify the dog before leaving on the real run.

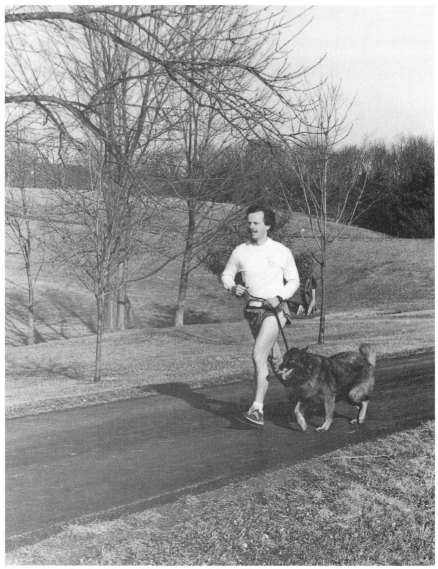

The author's husband, Brad, jogging with his Belgian Tervuren, Sabre.

As mentioned before, be careful about the heat when jogging. Increases in temperature decrease your dog's endurance faster than it does yours because his body does not cool as efficiently. He cannot sweat. When temperatures rise over 75 degrees, it is probably a good idea to leave your dog at home—even if that means you have to sneak out the door so that your canine jogging addict doesn't go berserk!

Be careful also as your distances increase that the pads on your dog's feet are up to it, especially if you run on hard surfaces. This is true whether you are jogging or walking your dog. Dogs' pads vary in their toughness; check the pads often. Hot pavement can blister a dog's feet. The road can remain hot even after the air has cooled.

The satisfaction some dogs derive from jogging transcends the exercise they receive. It is as if they have found the domestic equivalent of setting out on the hunt. A faraway look comes into their eyes; they ignore all distractions, intent on just covering ground. Dog and human become comrades in pursuit of their destination.

Other Alternatives

Riding a bike while your dog runs along beside you on leash is another alternative for providing your dog with exercise. It requires teaching your dog to heel with a bicycle, and must be done in places without much traffic, either vehicular or pedestrian. You should keep your speed at a comfortable pace for your dog, so he can keep up with you at a trot and not have to run. This could be done in a deserted parking lot in the evening. A German endurance test requires a dog to trot beside his owner on a bicycle for 12 miles, and then perform a few obedience exercises at the end of it. This test must be passed before a German Shepherd can be bred in Germany.

In hot weather, swimming is a good form of exercise. It is great exercise for older dogs with arthritis because the joints do not have to bear weight while they are being used. You will probably have to get into the water yourself

Biking a dog.

to teach your dog to enjoy swimming. While most dogs will swim if they fall into deep water, dogs will rarely step off into water over their heads to swim without encouragement from their owners. With a few lessons, however, they usually learn to love it. In our area, there are indoor swimming pools for dogs. One was previously used for rehabilitating injured racehorses.

If you cannot exercise your dog yourself, consider hiring a dog walker. You will miss out on the benefits to your relationship that exercising your dog provides, but at least your dog won't be frustrated. Your dog walker could be a neighborhood child who wants to earn some money. You can give your dog walker a prescribed route to follow for these walks, or he could just throw a ball for your dog in your backyard. This is a good alternative for a single person who works during the day and has occasional commitments in the evening that would preclude any time for walking a dog, or for an older person.

Although training does not have the same relaxing effects as other forms of exercise, it can tire out a rambunctious dog. There may be times that your dog needs to be exercised but you cannot go far from home. Just run through the exercises described in chapter 5. Do them at a brisk pace. If pouring rain makes the prospect of a walk less than thrilling, try training indoors. Heel around the dining room table. Practice your stays. Try leaving the room while your dog is on a down-stay. Take turns with another family member calling him from different rooms of the house. Teach him a trick. How about jumping a small barrier set up in a hallway or a doorway? Make sure you do this on a carpet so he doesn't slip.

Be creative in solving your exercise problems. For instance, if your dog likes to retrieve but you cannot throw a ball any distance, try hitting a tennis ball with a tennis racket. You can practice coming when called and exercise your dog at the same time if you have another person with whom to call your dog back and forth. Don't forget the food rewards! When we lived in Vermont and had to cope with a long winter, we exercised our dogs by taking them cross-country skiing.

I use a combination of ways to exercise my dogs. We are fortunate to have enough property for two 20-minute off-leash walks a day. I often invite other dogs to join us to increase the play. Once a week we try to go for a 45-minute hike in the woods. We drive to local state forests for these hikes. My husband often jogs with them once or twice a week for a couple miles. All of this does as much for our mental relaxation as for our dogs. You wouldn't want to be around me if I miss my daily dog walk. Agility training provides some exercise. A sewage treatment plant near us has lovely open fields with a creek for cooling off. Sometimes there is a bit of an odor, but the dogs don't mind. Now that's a creative solution to an exercise problem!

The Benefits of Exercise

This chapter has emphasized the behavioral reasons to exercise your dog, but there are many health reasons as well. Your dog's weight gives you a big clue about whether or not he is getting enough exercise. Just like people, dogs who get exercise and keep their weight down are healthier and live longer.

Exercising your dog can have special benefits just for you. It will force you to take a break from the frantic rush of modern life. The time that my husband and I spend exercising our dogs together is often our only chance for uninterrupted conversation. Exercising your dog will encourage you to get exercise that you might not get otherwise. Even though you are tired when you get home from work, walking your dog may be just the thing you need to wind down and relax.

There is something special about the bond you form with your dog when you exercise together. You are meeting one of his most basic needs. You are not making demands on him like you are when you are training him. It is quality time. Exercising your dog is an expression of your love for him.

Participating in an obedience class can be beneficial and fun for both you and your dog.

8

Common Behavior Problems

"Max, get down. Get down! Oh, no, my new silk dress is ruined."

"Honey, you better come into the living room. You're not going to believe what Toby did to the sofa."

"Hi. Come on in. I'll have to put Fifi in the bedroom so we can talk. She won't stop barking."

"Oh, Mitzi won't let you touch her. She doesn't like men, children, or women in hats."

If these lines sound familiar, maybe you have some of the behavior problems covered in this chapter: jumping up, destructive chewing, excessive barking, and shyness. Combined with housebreaking, not coming when called, pulling on leash, and biting, which are covered elsewhere in this book, these are the most common reasons people call me for help with their dogs. They are also the reasons many dogs are destroyed daily in animal shelters.

There are rarely quick fixes for behavior problems because these are usually symptoms of more complicated underlying problems that need to be solved, most involving miscommunication between owner and dog. If you haven't read the previous chapters, you will need to read chapter 1 to understand why punishment won't work and chapter 4 to understand the effects of your dog's personality on the problems you are having. The training described in chapter 5 is an important tool in solving any problem because it builds a foundation of communication. Armed with basic training and understanding, you can attack the problem. However, the discussions of the behavior problems presented here are by necessity simplified. Additionally, there are dog behavior problems that could not be covered. If this chapter does not help you solve your problem, do not hesitate to consult a professional.

Jumping Up

Jumping up is the behavior problem listed most frequently on the registration sheets for my obedience classes. It is a good behavior problem to have because it means you have a normal, friendly dog. I'd be concerned about the temperament of a dog, especially a puppy, who *didn't* want to jump up. As I said above, there is no magic cure for this problem, like stepping on his toes or hitting him in the chest with your knee. While these methods sometimes work, they can make your dog afraid of you, and they probably will not stop him from jumping up on other people. Instead, you should teach your dog how you want him to greet people, not violently punish him for greeting you or someone else in his own natural body language.

Your dog's personality will affect the degree of difficulty in training him not to jump up. Dogs who are excitable naturally find it difficult to control themselves in stimulating situations like their owner's return or meeting new people. High-energy dogs have the same problem of self-control. Lots of exercise will help these dogs with their jumping up problem. Some dogs are less athletic than others and are less apt to jump up. I get the most complaints from owners of Golden and Labrador Retrievers. The combination of size, energy level, and overwhelming friendliness makes jumping up a challenging problem for owners of these dogs to correct.

You cannot solve your jumping up problem without doing basic obedience training, so as a famous dog training saying goes, "Train; don't complain." Chapter 5 details this training. Start by perfecting the sit-stay for petting exercise from the basic training described in Week 1. Make sure your dog will consistently stay sitting when someone approaches him and pets him. This means he is doing it without being held in place with a tight leash or a death grip on his collar. He should be doing it in different places—at the door when company comes (as described in Week 4), outside in your yard, and when he meets people on walks.

While you are training him, it is a good idea to always have him on leash when people come to visit. Some people forget that leashes work just as well indoors as outdoors! Keep the leash close to the door so that it is handy when you need it. The slip lead described in chapter 5 works well for this. This makes it easy to correct him for jumping up, and you can keep him with you until he calms down. This is a necessity for an excitable dog. Your visitors will be grateful.

It is easy to get so involved with correcting your dog for jumping up that you forget to praise and reward him when he stays on the ground. This is a big mistake. Don't ignore him when he is patiently sitting in front of you. If the only time he gets your attention is when he jumps up, even though it is negative attention, he will keep jumping up. You must pet him and pay attention to him when he is not jumping up.

Consistency is essential for solving this problem. You cannot let your dog jump up sometimes and try to prevent him from doing so at others. This is a case where you need to discipline yourself, not your dog. If your dog is too excited when you get home or you are in too much of a rush to work on training, kneel down or bend over to pet him so he doesn't have to jump up to greet you. Don't come into your house with your hands full so you cannot prevent him from jumping up. Make two trips from your car so your hands are empty when you enter the house. Keep a container of treats outside your door, so you are ready to lure your dog into a sit and then reward him. Another strategy to distract your dog from jumping up is to throw a favorite toy or ball. You can also take a whole handful of dry dog food and throw it on the floor, so your dog is busy gobbling up food instead of mauling you or your guests.

Don't forget to provide your dog with lots of exercise. It is unfair to expect a dog who is ready to explode with energy not to jump up.

It is important if you are going to teach your dog not to jump up on other people that you don't isolate him. Before he is trained, it will seem easier to just put him outside or in another room, but he will never have an opportunity to learn that way, and the isolation will probably make him more excited and more likely to jump in the future. In fact, the more people he meets, the less excited he will be when meeting someone and therefore the less likely he will be to jump up. Take him places where he can meet lots of people. A favorite of mine is outside the main building of a local college when classes are changing. Almost every student stops to say hello and pat the dog, and by the hundredth student, the dog is too tired to jump up. Then you can praise and reward him for his good behavior.

Jumping up is a particularly difficult problem when small children are involved. Start by training your dog not to chase the children in the first place. Practice having your dog do a sit-stay and down-stay while the kids race around. Also practice using the "off" command with your dog on leash while the children jump around. Don't forget the praise!

Children over the age of four or five years can be taught to perform the come and sit exercise in order to encourage a dog to sit instead of jumping up on them. An adult should first teach the dog the exercise. Then the child should be taught how to get the dog to sit for food. Show the child how to make the hand motion to get your dog to sit and how to give a loud, firm command. If the child is young, hold his hand and guide it in the proper motion. Practice first without the dog. It will help if you tell the child to keep the piece of food closed in his fist, and not to open it and give it to the dog until you say to. He should open his hand flat to allow the dog to take the food. If he holds it in the tips of his fingers, he might get nibbled on and become frightened. It may be hard to overcome the child's natural tendency to jerk his hand away and try to hold it out of the dog's reach, but not doing so will just encourage the dog to jump more. An added advantage of working with a child on this exercise is that you are teaching your dog not to jump up and grab food out of a child's hand.

When the sitting is going well, add the come part. Practice calling the dog back and forth between you and the child, getting your dog to sit each time. If you have more than one child, play the run and freeze game. Have all the children run around with your dog. You yell, "Freeze," and the children have to stop. The child closest to your dog gets him to sit. Children learn they can control the chasing and jumping by freezing.

If you are reaching the point of desperation with this problem, and you have really worked hard on the obedience training, you can use a spray bottle filled with half water and half white distilled vinegar. This should be your last resort because it will punish your dog for being friendly. However, if your dog is hurting you or your children, the spray bottle is a good idea. It works well especially if your dog is jumping up and biting you at the same time. The vinegar mixture is more effective than just water, and it won't hurt your floors. It also won't hurt your dog's eyes, although he will blink fast enough to prevent that.

Here's how to use it. Give the "off" command first, and then spray him in the face. It is very important that you give the command first. Otherwise, he will never learn the command, and will behave only when you have the spray bottle. The spray bottle is much less damaging to your relationship than hitting your dog or otherwise hurting him to discourage jumping up.

The spray bottle is an especially good way for children to correct a dog because it does not involve any physical strength, but they must only be allowed to use it when directly supervised by an adult. The temptation to chase the dog around the house spraying him is too much for most children to resist. One client of mine found it useful in the mornings when the combination of a 12-week-old Golden Retriever puppy fresh from a night of sleep and three boys between the ages of 7 and 12 years rushing around to get off to school resulted in clothes being ripped and torn when the puppy jumped up to grab them. The boys used the spray bottle to discourage this bad habit.

There are probably times when you don't mind if your dog jumps up on you. Such enthusiastic expressions of love are hard to resist. Besides, it only seems fair to sometimes let him express himself in a way that is natural to him. It is okay to allow your dog to jump up on you when you invite him to do so. Establish a command or signal to let him know it is okay. You could just say "okay," his release word, or pat your body, or make an upward signal with your arms. In fact, a good way to teach your dog the meaning of the word "off" is to alternate inviting him to jump up, then saying "off" to tell him to get down.

A marvelous example of using a special command for jumping up was taught by a friend of mine to her huge male Irish Wolfhound named Milo. Jumping up takes on a new meaning when one is talking about the tallest breed of dog. Milo puts his paws on my shoulders and has to *bend down* to lick my face. Milo's command to jump up is, appropriately enough, "get tall."

Milo is beautifully trained and never jumps up without his command. He loves to do this so much that his owner uses it as a reward for training. I recently ran into my friend and Milo at a dog show. We don't see each other often because we live a distance apart, but Milo is always thrilled to see me. I kept him for a couple weeks as a favor to my friend when he was a very young puppy, so he regards me as his second mother. We couldn't let him "get tall" until I was done showing my dog and could suffer the damage to my clothes, so Milo impatiently waited for his command. When it finally came, I braced myself for receiving his 125 pounds and gave the command. The ensuing action attracted the attention of everyone in the vicinity, and Milo and I enjoyed expressing our deep affection for each other.

Milo, the Irish Wolfhound, "getting tall."

Attention-Getting Behaviors

Dogs get bored. They lie around most of the day doing nothing, often getting inadequate exercise and mental stimulation. If they have to, they will find ways to get our attention, and they will learn quickly that behaviors that annoy us work the best. Often these behaviors, like grabbing the dish towel or barking at us, worked well when they were puppies because we thought they were cute. We laughed at them. A year later, we are frustrated by the same behavior. Dogs, like children, will do bad things if necessary to get your attention. Be very careful that you are not rewarding unwanted attention-seeking behaviors with negative attention. Is your dog barking at you to get you to pay attention to him? Go shut yourself in another room; don't "bark" back at him. Take away the attention, rather than adding to it.

You do have to respond to your dog when he seeks your attention in appropriate ways. My Irish Setter is bored right now watching me type this. Occasionally she brings me a toy to play with. I stop and throw it for her for a few minutes. Avoid canine boredom with plenty of exercise and lots of training.

Stealing

One of the most common attention-getting behaviors is stealing. Bored and ignored dogs will grab something to start a chase game. It works especially well if the object he steals is worth over $100. Dogs love chase games and often play these games with other dogs. Wolves do this, too.

If your dog grabs something, you need to do the opposite of what he wants. **Do not chase him!** Do not try to tell him to drop it or tell him he is a bad dog. That's attention. Do not take even one step toward him or look at him. Silently walk away from him, get a treat in the kitchen, and make a trade. If you chase him or yell at him, you will be rewarding the behavior with attention, even if it is negative attention. Making a trade for a treat (use the lowest-power treat necessary) is less rewarding than the chase game. I know this seems like rewarding your dog for stealing, but it is the least rewarding thing that you can do to get back what he grabbed. Making a trade will avoid making your dog feel defensive and protective about an object he has stolen. In addition, this is a safe way for kids to get things away from dogs.

Your dog is going to keep trying to pick up your things unless he gets more attention for picking up his toys. Everyone's tendency when their dogs start to play with their own toys is to breathe a sigh of relief, try to get something else done, and ignore their dogs. You should do the opposite. When your dog picks up his toys, chase him around the dining room table and through the house. This way he is more likely to grab the squeaky dinosaur rather than the TV remote.

I must confess that my Irish Setter does on occasion grab a glove or a sock. She heads for the dog biscuit jar, sits, and waits for me to make a trade. I usually comply, even though she responds to a "drop it" command. I think it's kind of cute, and I'm happy she never destroys anything. If your dog is guarding an object and threatening you, do not confront him. Punishment will make your dog more defensive and more likely to bite the next time. Do what I describe above: make a trade. At first, you may have to use very powerful treats, especially if your dog has a history of being afraid of being punished. If he only guards certain objects, like rawhide bones, stop giving them to him. You should also read the section on "Dominance Aggression" in chapter 9 on aggression. You should also seek the help of a professional.

Teach your dog the "leave it" command as described in chapter 5 and use this command *before* your dog steals something. Don't forget to reward him for this.

Practice teaching "drop it" with objects your dog is likely to easily give up. Use treats. Sometimes ask your dog to drop something, pick it up, and then immediately give it back to him. If your dog likes to retrieve, use two balls to teach "drop it." Throw one ball, and then encourage him to come back by waving the second ball. When he gets back, tell him to "drop it," and don't throw the second ball until he does.

Of course, some dogs steal food off counters just because they'd like a snack. The best solution for this is not to leave food on counters! This is what microwaves are for: storing countertop food. The vinegar and water spray bottle sprayed at the second a dog sniffs the counter, before he even jumps up, works well. The best time to teach this is when puppies are young and impressionable, about 12 weeks old. You can find alarms in Radio Shack or dog supply catalogs that sense motion that can alert you to a sneaky dog.

Destructive Chewing and Separation Anxiety

Let's get one thing straight from the start: Dogs do *not* destroy things out of spite. Most of the time they do so to relieve tension caused by stress. Just as people sometimes smoke, eat, drink, or take drugs to cope with tension, dogs chew. The solution lies in relieving your dog's tension and unhappiness, and if that is not possible, in confining him to prevent further damage to your possessions and to himself.

You will notice that there is no mention of punishment for destructive chewing. The reason for this is illustrated by a story told in chapter 1. Most punishment for destructive chewing is given hours after the chewing has taken place, as dogs are usually most upset right after their owners leave. The dog doesn't understand why he is being punished, although some owners mistakenly assume their dogs know because they behave in a submissive manner. The dog acts afraid because his owner is angry, *not* because he knows he has done something wrong. Not only does punishment not work, it can actually make matters worse because it will make the dog more anxious and therefore more likely to chew in the future.

Like all behavior problems, destructive chewing is affected by your dog's personality. Different things stress dogs with different personalities. If your dog is dependent, he will be stressed by being left alone. A high-energy dog is stressed by lack of exercise. A highly reactive dog is stressed by too much stimulation.

To know how to work on chewing problems, you first need to figure out whether the chewing is caused by boredom or separation anxiety. A dog with separation anxiety will show signs of nervousness before you leave. He may follow you around, whining, panting, drooling, or trembling. He might howl and whine when you are gone. The destruction usually occurs around doors or windows. A dog might urinate or defecate in the house out of stress, although this may simply be a housebreaking problem. A dog with separation anxiety is truly panicked when you leave.

Separation anxiety can be a very difficult and time-consuming problem to solve. It's different from training your dog to do something; you are trying to change his emotional response when you leave. This means associating things like picking up your keys with treats. You can find more information on a program like this from a behavior specialist or a book on separation anxiety. If your dog is a "Velcro" dog, attached to you at all times, you can teach him a sit-stay and gradually increase the distance until you can go into another room. A truly terrified dog may need medications, but medications alone rarely help.

If your dog is chewing because he is bored, he will mostly choose fun things to chew on or things with your scent on them. He might tear apart a sofa cushion and enjoy scattering foam all over the living room, or using the TV remote as a chew toy. The solution to this kind of chewing, besides confining your dog while you are away, is to provide your dog with more exercise and mental stimulation. Provide him with a special distracting toy when you leave, something he doesn't get any other time. Try filling a Kong toy or hollow bone with squeeze cheese or peanut butter mixed with dog food. Take him on car rides with you. An obedience class based on positive reinforcement is great for mental stimulation. An agility class could combine both exercise and fast thinking for you and your dog! Your dog might benefit from a midday visit from a dog walker.

Some dogs with separation anxiety can tolerate the regular hours of separation that occur when their owners go to work, but are stressed if their owners leave them at unusual times, such as going out in the evening if they work during the day. Such dogs may need to be confined only during those unusual times.

Destructive chewing can be cause by fear, like fear of thunderstorms. This chewing will also be directed at doors or windows. Use a crate. Speak to your veterinarian about an anti-anxiety medication that may help, especially if he might injure himself in a crate.

Destructive chewing can also be caused by something happening outside the house that frustrates your dog, or even frightens him. The molding around a window can be destroyed because a car accident occurs outside the house while the owner is away and the dog is upset by all the commotion going on outside. If the chewing occurs near a door or window, look for something outside your house that is frustrating your dog. Are there squirrels playing outside where your dog can see them? Do many people walk dogs by your house? Is your dog afraid of loud noises that frighten him when he is home alone? My Greyhound offers a good example. While she is not at all upset if I drive away from the house, she is terribly frustrated if I go out to my dog training building, which is just 20 feet from my back door. From my bedroom window she can see into the window in the door of the building and catch glimpses of me as I move about. Her reaction is to grab a magazine lying on the nightstand and tear it to shreds. There are magazines lying all over the house in all sorts of accessible places, but these are the only magazines she ever touches. If this kind of frustration is causing your dog's destruction problem, either change what is happening outside or restrict your dog's ability to see outside.

Puppies chew out of curiosity and playfulness. Use a bottle of a bitter-tasting solution purchased at a pet supply store to discourage him from chewing. Spray it on furniture legs and tissues in the trash can. That way you will not have to get your relationship off to a bad start by constantly having to correct him. Confine your puppy when you are away, for his safety and the safety of your house. Your dog may be one to two years old before you can trust him loose in the house.

Dogs sometimes chew simply because they like to chew. They like to gnaw on something hard and to shred things into little pieces (causing the demise of many chair legs and foam pillows). Make sure your dog has plenty of safe things to chew. Mine seem to get a lot of satisfaction from something as simple as ripping apart an empty cardboard box. If you have any doubt about the safety of something you want to give your dog, such as rawhide bones, check with your veterinarian.

Finally, a behavior problem with a simple solution. Does your dog get into the trash? Put it away!

Excessive Barking

It is interesting that wolves rarely bark, while dogs often do. Of course, wolves do not have cats walking outside a fence just beyond their reach, nor do they have mailmen trespassing onto their territory on a daily basis. Barking seems to be a behavior born of the many frustrations experienced by dogs living in a domestic setting. Excessive barking is often a prelude to biting, so it is a problem to be taken seriously.

Many people are initially reluctant to correct their dog for barking because they appreciate the protection that barking affords. The security of having a dog that barks to warn you of intruders is desirable, but this barking should not be allowed to get out of control. What you want is for your dog only to bark at appropriate things, and then to stop barking on your command.

First of all, decide what you want your dog to bark at and correct him for barking at anything else. For instance, a small child going by your house on a bicycle hardly poses a threat and should not be barked at. However, barking at a deliveryman driving up your driveway is okay. Dogs who live in apartments should only bark when someone knocks on the door.

Then teach your dog to stop barking on your command. The command I use is "that's enough." Stopping the barking can be difficult. Start by calmly going to your dog and taking hold of his collar. If the barking was appropriate, praise him with a quiet "good boy." Then say, "That's enough." If he doesn't stop, give him a firm shake with the collar, repeating, "That's enough." You can also try grabbing his muzzle with your right hand and pushing it down while you pull up on his collar with the left hand. The second he stops barking, *praise*. You could even give him a food reward. He may resume barking immediately. Repeat the command and correction until he stops.

If your dog's barking has reached the point of hysteria, you might want to try the spray bottle technique described above in the section on jumping up. As before, fill it with a 50-50 mixture of distilled white vinegar and water. Give the command to stop barking, then spray him in the face. He is bound to stop, if only for a millisecond, but be sure to praise him when he does.

You can stop a dog's barking by pushing down on his muzzle while pulling up on his collar.

By teaching your dog to stop barking on command, you are preventing the barking from escalating to biting. Many people do not see the relationship between barking and biting and are surprised when their out-of-control barkers bite someone. The purpose of barking is to warn off intruders; if that doesn't work, biting is sometimes the next step the dog will take.

To keep barking under control, every time your dog barks you must go check it out, praise him for barking if it was appropriate, and then tell him to stop. Recently, I was too lazy to check to see what my Irish Setter, Kyra, was barking at. I told her to stop. When she didn't, I went to her and gave her a shake with the collar. The now hysterical barking continued. Finally, I looked out the window, expecting to see a stray cat. Much to my shock, there was a bear outside my door! I learned my lesson.

If your dog is barking when he is outside, either in a fenced yard or on a chain, he is doing so because he is frustrated. The best way to solve the problem is to reduce your dog's frustration. The easiest way may be to simply keep your dog inside and only allow him out when you are with him or for short periods, not long enough to become bored and frustrated. You can also change the environment somehow, with plants, privacy fencing, or vinyl strips woven into the fencing to reduce the visibility of whatever causes your dog's frustration and barking. If he barks when he is outside with you, correct the same way you would if he were inside. Do not allow the frustration to build, especially if the barking is at people or children, because the dog may eventually bite in frustration.

Another tool for stopping unwanted barking is a citronella spray bark collar. These collars emit a puff of citronella spray from a box on the collar. The puff hits under a dog's chin and startles him rather than hurting him. It may take several puffs before your dog figures it out. Be careful that a sensitive dog may be very frightened by the puff spray.

If the reason your dog is frustrated and barking is that he is isolated in the backyard, solve the problem that caused you to isolate him in the first place so that he can have some much-needed companionship.

Shyness

Shyness, or fear of people, is a serious problem because if a dog becomes fearful enough, he may bite. This problem is commonly referred to as fear biting. If you see shyness in a puppy, even if he is as young as five weeks, don't count on him growing out of it and start working on it right away. In less severe cases of shyness, good training can almost completely make the problem disappear. For instance, as I indicated in chapter 1, my first dog, an Irish Setter, was shy. We struggled in our first obedience class trying to persuade her to allow the instructor to touch her. After she was obedience trained, no one would believe that she had ever been shy. She visited nursing homes and schools regularly to put on obedience demonstrations, always allowing everyone to pet her afterward. More severe cases of shyness respond less dramatically to training, but usually there is some improvement.

Shyness can either be genetic or caused by a lack of socialization when the dog is a puppy. The hereditary version can be found in all breeds of dogs as well as mixed breeds. The widespread nature of this problem is understandable if you look at the heritage of the dog before it was domesticated. Wolves, a close relative of the dog, are timid and shy by nature. This is a helpful adaptation for their survival. Domestication has reduced this shyness in dogs, but the trait can still be present in their genes and can often appear when dogs are bred indiscriminately. An inherited shyness problem can be improved greatly with training, but it cannot be totally erased.

The other cause of shyness is a lack of socialization. Dogs that do not receive adequate human contact between the ages of 5 and 12 weeks are usually shy of humans. This can happen when puppies are raised outside in a barn or kennel, or in a puppy mill situation. This shyness can also be improved with training, but you can never completely compensate for the lack of socialization. Shyness of strange people and places can also occur if a puppy is only exposed to the people who own him and the place where he lives until the age of 16 weeks.

When people get shy dogs from animal shelters, they often assume that it is the result of previous abuse. While abuse can cause shyness, such shyness quickly fades when the dog is placed in a loving, understanding, and consistent environment. If shyness persists in such dogs, it is probably a congenital problem, not the result of abuse. Dogs also do not become permanently shy from one traumatic incident, such as being roughly handled by a veterinarian or groomer. A dog with a good, stable temperament cannot be changed into a shy dog with one incident.

Some dogs also exhibit shyness when they enter their adolescence, somewhere around the age of six to nine months, even though they have never shown any previous shyness problems. The stress of hormonal changes probably has something to do with this. Treat this type as you would any other form of shyness, but be especially careful to avoid forcing your dog into a situation that is too stressful for him to handle. By doing so you could turn a temporary problem into a permanent one.

No matter what the cause of shyness, a friendly obedience class based on positive reinforcement is a great help. (See chapter 10 for how to find a good class.) Try to find a class taught by someone experienced in handling shy dogs. By going to a class, a shy dog gets to meet people and other dogs in a strange place but in a controlled situation. He gets to see the same people and dogs every week, which helps him to become gradually less frightened. Being told specifically what to do and how to behave also helps him cope with a frightening situation. The praise and treats he will get as he learns will make him feel good about himself. He will learn to tolerate the instructor petting him while he is made to stay. In many ways, a class can be a confidence-building experience for a shy dog.

The most important tool to use in helping a shy dog is food. You want to pair the "scary" thing with a good thing. No biscuits here. Get out the power food. Some nice cubes of hard salami work well.

Start working on your shyness problem by using food at whatever level your dog is comfortable. Shy dogs are more comfortable approaching someone on their own than being approached, so you want to start by teaching your dog to approach people to get a treat. If you hold a dog tightly by the leash or collar to force him to let people pet him, he will feel cornered because he cannot escape and will be more afraid. This can lead to a bite. If your dog is so afraid that he will not approach a person to take food from their hand, start by having that person sit on the floor and toss food to the dog, gradually decreasing the distance that the food is thrown until the dog is taking a piece of food from the person's hand outstretched at arm's length. I like using squeeze cheese spread on my hand, so the dog can't grab the food and back away. He has to stay with me to lick my hand.

Continue training your dog by encouraging him to approach people offering him food. *Don't forget to praise him whenever he acts in a friendly, confident manner.* When he will readily approach someone holding out a piece of food, start having people do the approaching while your dog is on a sit-stay.

Take advantage of any and every opportunity to have someone strange feed your dog. Carry treats with you when you go for walks to hand to people. You want your dog to think that everyone he meets is a potential source of treats, rather than a threat.

It is critical in dealing with this problem not to unintentionally reward your dog for acting shy and make the problem worse. When your dog is afraid of someone, it is natural to try to reassure him. However, he has no way of understanding that your reassurance is regarding the person. Instead, he will think your soft words and petting are an expression of approval for his fearful behavior. This is certainly not what you want to teach him. An example of this is given in chapter 3 in "Building Confidence."

What you want to communicate to your dog instead is that he is acting silly and that you are not going to tolerate it. Speak firmly to him in a no-nonsense tone of voice. If he is a little dog, do not pick him up and cuddle him. Don't let him lean on you or hide behind you. Rather, place him on a sit-stay on your left side and stubbornly make him stay there. If the most he can tolerate at first is a person walking around him in a circle, staying 10 feet away, start there. Then gradually work up to having him sit and stay while an unfamiliar person approaches him and hands him a piece of food. When your dog is comfortable with this, make him do a sit-stay while the person approaches and pets him *before* giving him the food reward. You will know

Offering a shy dog food will help him overcome his fear of people. (Mixed Breed)

you really have your problem under control when you can leave your dog on a sit stay, go 6 feet away, and have a stranger pet your dog without you standing right next to him for security.

You will need to get your shy dog out and exposed to people and places. Be very careful so that you do not put your dog in a situation where he is so afraid that he feels forced to bite to defend himself. Watch your dog carefully for any signs that he is feeling uncomfortable and remove him from the situation before he becomes frightened. While shy dogs need encouragement to face their fears, there is a point at which you can stress them too much and cause them to become more fearful. It is important to read your dog so that you know when to stop. Watch the expression in his eyes as well as the tenseness of his muscles. If he refuses to eat his treats, that is a sign that he is stressed.

If your dog's shyness or fear causes him to growl or bite, please see the next chapter on aggression and seek the help of an experienced trainer or behavior specialist. A good trainer can lay out a detailed program using positive reinforcement for desensitization and counter-conditioning.

One final thought: Do not breed from a shy dog. It is impossible to know for sure if a dog is shy because of a genetic problem that he can pass on to offspring or if this condition was caused by a lack of socialization. There is no way to go back and see if your dog would have had a good temperament if he had received adequate socialization. And please do not use the excuse that your dog is shy because of a traumatic incident to justify breeding a shy dog. It is irresponsible to take a chance on producing another generation of shy puppies when the world is grievously overpopulated with dogs.

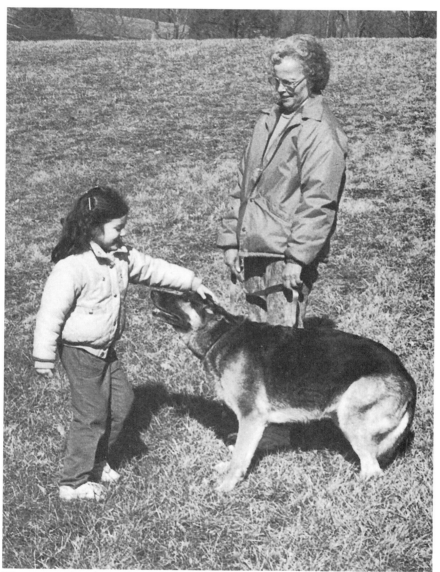

Whenever a dog shows fear in his body language, owners should be aware of the potential for dog bites. (German Shepherd)

9

Aggression

People never call me and say that they have a biting problem with their dog. Instead, the usual phone call goes something like this:

Owner: "Hello. I think my dog needs some training."
Me: "What problems are you having?"
Owner: "Well, he doesn't like some people."
Me: "What do you mean by not liking people?"
Owner: "He just doesn't like some people."
(By now I guess that there is a problem the owner is having trouble admitting to, and that getting information is going to be like pulling teeth.)
Me: "Has he ever bitten anyone?"
Owner: "Well, he once snapped at a man he didn't like."
Me: "Did he bite the man?"
Owner: "Well, sort of."
Me: "Was the skin broken?"
Owner: "Yes."
Me: "Did it require stitches?"
Owner: "Yes, a few."
Me: "How many?"
Owner: "Well, ten, but this is the only person he's bitten that had to go to the hospital. He's really a nice dog most of the time."

You may laugh, but I am not exaggerating. One of the most dangerous things about dog aggression problems is that people often deny that the problem exists until it is fairly advanced and therefore harder to solve or, even worse, until someone is badly bitten. The purpose of this chapter is to help you recognize if your dog has an aggression problem and to help you understand it. It is *not* about how you can solve your dog's aggression problem. Diagnosing and solving this kind of problem, if it can be solved, generally requires expert help.

There are many reasons people might deny that their dog has an aggression problem. Many people like their dog's protectiveness until it gets out of control and becomes a liability. Some owners blame their dog's aggression on abuse the dog might have suffered before he came to live with them, and they hope that love will cure it. Others think it is just puppy behavior and that their dog will grow out of it as he matures. People may put off seeking help because it is hard to admit that they are afraid of their dog. A common excuse is to blame the victim for provoking the dog, even if the provocation was a nonthreatening act, such as petting the dog.

"But he's nice most of the time." This is a statement I often hear when dog owners contact me about their dog's aggression problem, and it explains why it is hard for owners to face their dog's problem. Their dogs *are* affectionate, cute, and playful some of the time, with some people. The owners love their dogs. The incidents of aggressive behavior occur infrequently at first, so it is easy to make excuses for a few nasty encounters until someone gets hurt. Oftentimes the owners don't even realize that they are learning what to do to avoid "setting the dog off," and they deceive themselves into thinking that he is getting better.

Biting, snapping, and growling are behaviors that can have many different causes. A dog may snap and growl as a form of play, or he may do it because he has some form of brain damage. Understanding the cause of aggressive behavior is important in deciding how to handle it. Here is a partial list of things that may cause aggressive behavior toward humans:

- fear (which can be caused by many things)
- protection of territory
- possessiveness of an object
- protection of a litter of puppies
- dominance aggression
- abuse
- pain
- objection to being restrained
- interpreting punishment as an attack
- a drug side effect
- being raised without littermates or without a mother to teach inhibition of aggression

Because a dog cannot talk and tell you why he is biting, determining the cause requires good detective work: adding together the clues given by the dog's body language and behavior, asking the right questions about the dog's behavior, obtaining a thorough history of the dog's problem and upbringing, and looking at the dog's breeding. While an expert is best at preparing such a profile, this chapter should help you start to understand dog aggression problems.

Although some general patterns will be described, aggression problems cannot be easily categorized. All dogs are individuals with different backgrounds, both genetically and environmentally, that affect the problem. No two aggression problems are exactly alike. To complicate the situation, a dog may have more than one kind of aggression problem. Aggression against humans and aggression directed at other dogs are two separate problems, although both may exist in one dog.

The first and major part of this chapter will concentrate on aggression against humans because as an obedience instructor I receive more complaints about this kind of aggression. Aggression with other dogs will be discussed at the end of the chapter.

Keep in mind as you read about aggression that the really remarkable thing about dogs in general is not how aggressive they can be, but how gentle and willing to inhibit their bites they are.

Dog Personality Types and Aggression

Almost any dog will bite if stressed severely enough, but dogs with some personality types are more likely to bite than others. Among the personality factors that increase the likelihood that a dog will bite are breed predisposition, aggressive defense reactions, assertiveness, and excitability (see chapter 4 for more about these personality factors).

Some breeds were developed to bite and behave aggressively as part of their job. These include the herding breeds, terriers, and guarding breeds. Other breeds have had aggressive tendencies purposely bred out of them. For instance, I rarely see biting problems in Golden Retrievers and Siberian Huskies; aggression would be detrimental to both of these breeds' work patterns. Knowing your breed's aggression potential can alert you to early signs of an aggression problem so that it can be better managed. Since Lhasa Apsos may seem like lapdogs and Dalmatians like spotted clowns, ignorance of the protective behavior bred into these breeds may lead owners to overlook problems until someone is bitten. Of course, these are generalizations, and there is much variation among individuals within a breed.

As noted in chapter 4, some dogs will respond to stress, especially when frightened or cornered, by biting, while others will remain passive. Such aggressive defense reactions can become worse as a dog learns that they do indeed provide a good defense. Whenever dealing with dogs of this personality type, avoid confrontations that may cause the dog to bite. You don't want to give him the opportunity to learn the effectiveness of biting.

A dog with aggressive defense reactions may respond to punishment by growling or biting. He may interpret some kinds of punishment as an attack against which he has to defend himself. If so, change the punishment, or eliminate it. Any punishment in which anger is an overriding emotion, or lasts more than a few seconds, not to mention punishment that takes the form more of a beating than a reprimand, is likely to be misunderstood by a dog.

The assertive dog may let you know he is annoyed by something with a growl or bite. This can be seen in a seven-week-old puppy. There is no need to panic. It doesn't mean you have a vicious dog. It does mean you have to control this tendency. Your dog has the right to express himself, but he does not have the right to escalate that expression into greater aggression. If you bother your dog by petting him when he is exhausted and trying to sleep, and he growls to let you know it, there is no need for punishment. But take note of such a reaction, and make sure he will let you handle him when you have to. If the assertive aggressiveness of an adolescent male dog with his increased levels of testosterone becomes a problem, he will benefit from neutering. The resultant reduction in sexual tension will help him relax.

A dog who is excitable, or highly reactive to stimulation, may or may not have a tendency to bite. They are two separate characteristics. A dog may be very difficult to provoke because he is not excitable, but when he finally is sufficiently provoked, he will respond by biting. This would be typical of some large, heavy-boned member of the guard breeds. On the other hand, a very excitable Labrador Retriever may never defend himself by biting, no matter how much he is provoked. However, an excitable dog with aggressive tendencies, such as a nervous German Shepherd who is quick to snap, can be dangerous if not carefully supervised.

While personality factors are inherited and hard to change, early recognition of aggressive tendencies and appropriate training can prevent aggression problems from developing.

Does Your Dog Have an Aggression Problem?

The first step in dealing with your dog's aggression problem is deciding whether he has one. This is confusing because some aggression is considered acceptable and even desirable in dogs. In fact, probably an important reason dogs were domesticated was their instinctive ability to warn their human owners of intruders and drive the intruders away. Guarding has always been a valued characteristic of dogs.

In deciding if your dog has an aggression problem, it is not a question of what is normal or natural aggression for a dog, but what is acceptable to the human society in which dogs live. In most cases, the only legally and socially acceptable provocations for biting that relieve an owner of liability are

You should be able to take a rawhide bone away from your dog. (German Shepherd)

illegal trespassing on the dog owner's property; attacking the owner; or kicking, teasing, or in some other way tormenting the dog. While it may be natural for a dog to want to drive away all strangers that come into his territory, or to defend himself against the man in the white coat who attacks him with needles and thermometers, such behaviors cause problems in the dog-human relationship.

The following is a list of signals that your dog may have an aggression problem. If your answer is yes to any of these questions, you should seek help.

1. Has your dog ever snapped at or bitten anyone except under circumstances involving the provocations listed above?
2. Has your dog ever growled or snapped at you when you tried to discipline him?
3. Has your dog ever growled or snapped at you when you tried to take something away from him?
4. Do you avoid touching your dog in certain ways because you are afraid you will irritate him?
5. Does your dog snap at you when you try to brush him?
6. Has a groomer complained to you about having difficulty handling your dog?
7. Has your dog tried to snap at your veterinarian?

8. Does your dog bark hysterically when someone either comes to the house or goes by your house? Can you easily stop your dog from barking in these situations?

9. Does your dog growl at people after they enter your home, continue barking at them, or shy away from them?

10. Does your dog shy away from strangers when they try to touch him?

11. Do you not trust your dog around strangers?

12. Do you find yourself making excuses for your dog's hostile behavior?

13. Is your dog less than six months old and already acting hostile toward strangers?

Some signs are harder to see than others, but no matter what the signs are, you can always make excuses. Don't deny an aggression problem.

Head Collars and Aggression

Head collars (discussed in chapter 5) are useful in controlling an aggressive dog. If your dog lunges, whether at people or at other dogs, the head collar is definitely the best way to restrain him. The reason is not just the ease of preventing a lunge, but also that you can turn the dog's head away from the object of his aggression, breaking eye contact. For many dogs, breaking eye contact stops the aggressive behavior. Beware the use of a prong collar, which can increase aggression by adding pain to an already highly aroused dog. A head collar will not cure an aggression problem, but it is a useful tool.

Fear Aggression

Fear, whether caused by a lack of socialization or a genetic shyness, can cause a dog to bite. It is the aggression problem I see most frequently. Shyness is a common temperament problem in dogs, and people often inadvertently make the shyness worse by unintentionally rewarding their dog for shy behavior, as was described in chapters 3 and 8. Such rewarding can turn shyness into fear biting.

Fear aggression can progress to the point where a dog will attack to prevent an approach. Because the dog is initiating the attack, it is hard to see the fear behind it. Since looking at a dog usually precedes an approach, some dogs will attack when eye contact is made. I once worked with a dog who would growl if you made eye contact with him when he was 30 feet away. He put on quite a ferocious display if you approached closer. One time, in the middle of an aggressive lunge, his leash snapped. It was apparent that these attacks were meant to drive people away rather than attack them because he almost stopped in midair and ran back to hug his owner's side. Such behavior always reminds me of the Cowardly Lion in *The Wizard of Oz*. This is the best way to tell if the aggression you are seeing in a dog is based on fear. When a dog with this problem lunges forward to snap at someone, he quickly withdraws.

Treating fear aggression starts by treating the underlying shyness. Some techniques for this were described in chapter 8 in "Shyness." Don't try to have strangers pet your dog while you restrain him. He'll be more frightened because he can't escape and will feel cornered. If your dog lunges to bite, you will not be fast enough to stop him.

A common mistake is to misinterpret fear biting as overprotectiveness. The typical scenario is a dog pressed close against his owner, growling and baring his teeth at someone approaching, while the owner attempts to soothe the dog. The owner thinks the dog is protecting her, when in reality the dog is hoping the owner will protect him! Meanwhile, the owner's attempts to reassure her dog only serve to reward him for his aggressive behavior. The problem gets worse, until the dog darts forward and nips someone. The belief in the dog's "protectiveness" is reinforced by the fact that the dog displays the most or sometimes the only aggression when he is with his owner—not because he is protecting his owner, but because his owner's support gives him the false courage he needs to attack. In this situation, the owner's attitude is often the hardest problem to correct because the idea of being protected by one's dog is so gratifying. The owner may make halfhearted attempts to correct his dog, but the dog will interpret his owner's body language and will know what the real story is.

Dogs can be fear-aggressive of things other than strange people. As with shyness, these problems are treated by pairing the thing a dog is afraid of with something the dog loves, like freeze-dried liver.

An example was an Afghan I worked with who was afraid of grooming. This dog had become horribly matted to the point that his skin was irritated and he couldn't move his legs freely. Of course, the owners were terribly irresponsible to let this happen. He had snapped at the owners when they tried to brush him, so they avoided grooming. They tried taking him to a groomer, but he was too aggressive. He would attack at the sight of a brush because it had caused him so much pain. The owners were going to have him anesthetized to cut off his coat, but anesthesia is risky with sighthound breeds.

We started by placing scissors on the floor next to his food bowl at home when he ate. Then, when he came for a lesson, I placed the scissors six feet away from me and fed him when he approached. He was not restrained on leash, as that would have made him more frightened. He could choose to approach on his own. We continued until I could hold the scissors in the air close to him. I was finally, over several sessions, able to cut off all of his mats, which was most of his coat. He was never restrained for this. That is the power of positive reinforcement.

Territorial Aggression

As mentioned in an earlier part of this chapter, the trait of territorial protective aggression has been valued in dogs since their domestication, and selectively bred for. This trait varies tremendously in dogs, from dogs who show absolutely no protectiveness to others who gladly attack to defend their territory and try to keep enlarging the territory they defend.

The development of territorial protectiveness in dogs is linked to sexual maturity. A dog is most easily guided into appropriate but not excessive protective behavior if the protectiveness is addressed at the time it first appears. Owners of protective dogs have a responsibility to teach their dogs the limits of their protectiveness. Don't be reticent about putting limits on your dog's protectiveness for fear that he will cease all protection. You want to teach him what you consider threatening and what you do not. You also want to teach him that when you are home you will make the decision about who is permitted in your house and who is not.

As described in chapter 8, barking problems are warnings of territorial protection problems. By controlling a dog's excessive barking, the owner takes the first step toward solving a territorial protection problem.

It is important to note that if you think you are seeing protectiveness in a dog of less than six months of age, it is likely that what you really are seeing is fear aggression. One way to differentiate fear aggression from protective aggression is to evaluate the dog's response in various settings. The protective dog is friendly to strangers when out of his territory, even though

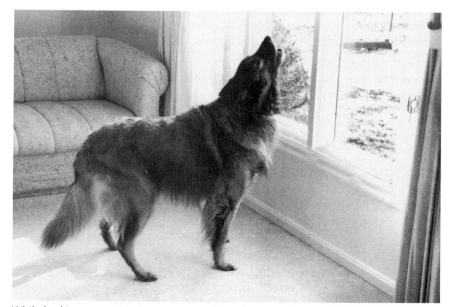

While barking a warning is a trait most dog owners welcome, allowing territorial aggression to get out of control can lead to problems. (Belgian Tervuren)

he is accompanied by his owner. The fearful dog behaves aggressively toward strangers anywhere.

Another mistake that people make with regard to protectiveness is the myth perpetuated by television and literature that dogs naturally protect their owners. Dogs will instinctively protect their territory, mostly preferring to drive intruders away rather than engage in a confrontation. They will protect themselves and their food and toys, but they rarely protect people, with the exception of when a child becomes a puppy substitute and is protected by a dog. Dogs are trained to attack people (and note that training is required to get a dog with a good temperament to attack people) by forcing the dog to attack to defend himself, or by making use of his instinct to kill prey.

Dogs will guard their owners as a source of affection and food, much as they would guard a bone. Some owners mistake this for protectiveness. Dogs direct this kind of aggression at people and other dogs. Typically, the dog will be sitting on the owner's lap being petted when someone nonthreatening approaches. The dog then growls at the person to keep them away. The owner should promptly dump the dog off their lap, rather than being flattered by this behavior. This behavior can also look like jealousy, especially when a dog growls at another dog to keep him away from the owner's attention.

The perfect guard dog is one who is confident around people and not afraid of them. In fact, he is very friendly with people. He barks when someone strange comes onto your property, but ignores children riding by on bicycles. He stops barking on your command, but continues to keep a watchful eye. If you say someone at your door is okay, he willingly makes friendly overtures to him or her. He would not allow anyone to enter your house when you are not home except for a few friends or family members he knows well. You feel secure when you are alone at home that you will be alerted if someone arrives, yet you are never afraid that your dog will bite someone when you have company. Because he is not afraid of people, if he ever does have to defend his territory, he won't hesitate. This kind of dog is the product of the right breed, good breeding, and good training.

When Fear Aggression and Territorial Aggression Combine

This is a very dangerous combination. It is the most common cause of dog bites to strangers that I see. If a dog is just fearful, he hides and avoids confrontations. If a dog is just territorial, he barks at strangers, but easily makes friends later. If your dog barks and growls, backing away from the stranger, and will not relax, you probably have a combination of both problems. This is important to know because both problems must be worked on separately.

Be very careful with this dog. He may avoid a stranger for a while in your house, and then bite the person when he moves. Put this dog on leash or confine him, especially if you are having many visitors and you will be too busy to watch him. A Gentle Leader, which is a head collar, is good for this problem. You may have to choose between losing your homeowners insurance or your dog if he bites.

A Word about Attack Trained Dogs

Although I don't remember where I read it, I remember another dog trainer making a very good point about the general public owning dogs trained to attack. He (or she) said that since most people cannot reliably make their dogs sit and stay, the idea of such people owning a dog trained to attack is frightening. If you feel that your home needs more protection, buy a burglar alarm. It is more reliable, and it won't attack the wrong person.

Dominance Aggression

When owners call and say that their dogs get a funny look in their eyes and then attack for no reason, I suspect dominance aggression. Dominance aggression is mainly directed at family members. These aggressive behaviors can be growling, snapping, or biting. This problem is not caused by owners, although what they do can make it better or worse. A dog is born with this problem. Ninety-five percent of the dogs with this are males. It can occur in any breed, from Shih Tzu to Golden Retriever to Rottweiler. Castration helps but does not solve the problem. Generally, the dog is fine as a puppy, but aggressive behaviors, starting with growling, begin around 12 to 18 months of age. Often the first biting episode occurs between 2 and 3 years old.

Although dominance aggression is the term that is popularly used for this problem, it is somewhat confusing. Dogs who have dominance aggression are not trying to dominate their owners; they just become very anxious about being dominated. It is an anxiety problem. These dogs react to owner behaviors that they consider dominating, and growl or bite to stop them.

Owners of dogs with this problem often report that their dogs bite for no reason. Actually, they just don't understand the triggers. These are common triggers for dominance aggressive dogs:

- Punishing the dog, either verbally or physically
- Touching the dog while he is lying down
- Attempting to control the dog by grabbing the collar
- Pushing the dog away, off your lap, or off the sofa or bed
- Reaching over the dog's head to pet him
- Trying to take away a bone or rawhide chew

An important sign that a dog has dominance aggression is that punishment makes it worse. Dogs increase their aggressive behavior as they are punished. Owners of these dogs either avoid punishing them or use objects such as newspapers so they can punish without being bitten.

This problem cannot be cured by training. Owners can only manage it and must face difficult decisions regarding the safety of family members, particularly if children are involved. Management involves avoiding things that trigger the dog, avoiding punishment and confrontations, and training the dog with positive reinforcement. Some behavioral specialists recommend drug treatment.

This is a horrible problem for owners to have. These dogs are often very intelligent and trainable, and are affectionate most of the time. They are happy to see their owners when they come home. Their owners love them. However, they can be very dangerous and cause injury to their owners.

Earlier in my career as a dog trainer, I tried to train these dogs. Working with these owners, I was able to make an improvement in the dog's behavior. However, when I checked with these owners after a year, nearly all of the dogs had bitten again. These incidents were always described as occurring without warning or provocation. In two cases, children were bitten badly enough to need several stitches. I learned through experience that training does not cure this problem; it only manages it and gives the owners a false sense of security. After careful evaluation to determine that this is indeed the type of aggression the dog has, I no longer attempt to train dogs with bad cases, and recommend euthanasia because of the dangers involved.

This behavior problem is one that causes an owner to get rid of his dog, whether by taking his dog to a shelter, giving him to a rescue group, or abandoning the dog. Be aware that this problem can show up in dogs that you may adopt. If a dog has had several homes, be suspicious.

Dogs Aggressive with Strange Dogs

There are several reasons that dogs are aggressive with strange dogs. Some are frustrated by their lack of opportunity to play with other dogs, so they lunge and bark. Some dogs are afraid of other dogs due to lack of socialization and growl to keep them away. Other dogs have had traumatic experiences with other dogs, and some were removed from their litter too early. With some dogs you may never know the reason because they were rescued at an older age. If your dog responds aggressively only to obnoxious behavior from another dog, he is just behaving normally. (More on this below.)

Is your dog lunging at strange dogs when you take him for walks? The first thing you need to do is arm yourself with a bag of delicious treats and a head collar, such as a Gentle Leader. Your goal should not be to make your dog friendly with other dogs. Just like people, not all dogs get along. Your goal should be to have your dog walk politely by another dog, keeping his attention on you. Start feeding your dog the minute you spot another dog, before your dog sees the other dog, and keep feeding him until the other dog is past. Use your Gentle Leader to break eye contact with the other dog. No Gentle Leader? Just turn around abruptly and head in the other direction. Another useful tool is the vinegar and water spray bottle (described in chapter 8), used just as your dog sees another dog and *before* he lunges or barks. It is beyond the scope of this book to describe a complete desensitization and counter-conditioning program.

Dogs who bark wildly at the window when another dog walks by are not only being annoying; they are the dogs who are likely to get into a fight if they escape out the door, or worse, run across a street to chase a dog and get hit by a car. These dogs have a mistaken sense of power because they think they are driving other dogs away with their barking. You need to stop this behavior, and you need to do more than just yell at him, which you've probably already discovered doesn't work. Try something as simple as calling him when he starts to bark and giving him a treat for coming. You might also try the spray bottle. If your dog is just mildly aggressive, try an obedience class. That way he'll learn to listen around other dogs. Bring powerful treats to keep his attention. Some dogs, however, are too aggressive to be in a class with other dogs. Be honest with the instructor or training club when you sign up. Perhaps you can take a few private lessons before going into a class.

Using a spray bottle to correct barking. (Border Terrier)

Normal Aggressive Response to Rude Dogs

Here's a news flash: dogs can't talk. If another dog is bothering them, they can't tell them to back off, so they tell them by lunging and snapping at them. Some dogs are more intolerant of other dogs' obnoxious behavior than other dogs. That's okay. Don't punish your dog. It's your job to protect your dog from rude and obnoxious dogs. Rude dogs are ones who run up to your dog, get in his face, and maybe jump on him. They are overly friendly and rough.

My husband and I have just added an eight-week-old Belgian Tervuren puppy to our household. Rude doesn't even begin to describe his behavior with our older Irish Setter. When she finally has had enough of him hanging off her long ears and beautiful tail, she lunges at him and snaps. And you know what I do? I praise her. She needs my emotional support. While it is frightening to see a tiny puppy snapped at, it is the only way she has of telling him "no." Now if I can just learn to communicate with him as effectively as she does!

Dogs Who Are Aggressive with Other Dogs in the Household

This is a phone call I am always unhappy to receive because there is often nothing I can do to solve the problem. Once two dogs in the same household decide to hate and mistrust each other, it is hard to change them. These problems most often occur between two dogs of the same sex, either male or female, who have not been neutered or spayed. They can occur, however, between any two dogs. Often they are struggling over dominance. When two dogs are of equal dominance, it is hard for that struggle to be resolved. It is heartbreaking when this problem emerges when one of the dogs reaches maturity at one to two years of age, as often happens. By then, the owners are attached to both dogs. Fights can result in injuries to both dogs.

Do not attempt to figure out which dog started the fight and punish him. You will not be able to read the subtle body language that occurs in these encounters. Sometimes dog-to-dog aggression problems are solved with good management and good training. Make sure both dogs listen to basic obedience commands. Don't throw one toy for both dogs to retrieve if they are competitive. Supervise playtime to make sure play doesn't escalate into fighting. Be careful about feeding times. Make sure nobody switches to another dog's bowl. Train your dogs to wait their turn to receive treats. Make everyone sit first.

Finding Help

If you think your dog has an aggression problem, you need to get expert help, but it probably won't be easy to find. Anyone can call himself an animal behavior consultant or dog psychologist. There are no licensing requirements. This is complicated by the fact that someone with a Ph.D. in animal behavior may have little practical experience in handling aggressive dogs, while a dog trainer with no academic degrees may have a lot of experience and be of great help.

You can ask a veterinarian for referrals; however, be cautious about taking your veterinarian's advice regarding your dog's aggression problem unless he has had special training in this area beyond the normal veterinary training. His advice may be well meaning but lacking a foundation in experience and knowledge. You could also contact the nearest veterinary school for a referral. They often have a dog behavior specialist on staff.

Taking an obedience class might be helpful if your aggression problem has not progressed far and if your dog is young. If you sign up for a class, tell the instructor about your aggression problem beforehand. Be honest with him or her. The instructor may not feel qualified to handle your problem, or may feel that the class setting is inappropriate for your dog. He or she may require that you take some private lessons before entering a class.

When dealing with an aggression problem, don't add tension to tension, or aggression to aggression. If your dog is tense and in a situation in which you think he may bite, you will only increase the likelihood of that happening if you become tense yourself. Your dog will sense your fears and become more stressed himself, feeling more of a need to defend himself. Instead, try relaxing your dog with happy talk, play, and laughter. Don't increase your dog's aggression by adding aggression with punishment that is hostile in nature, excessive, and beyond the point of instructional correction.

Conclusion

This chapter has given a simplified overview of a very complex problem, and has only touched on the more common kinds of aggression problems. As previously mentioned, all dogs are individuals, making every aggression problem different and not easily categorized.

If your dog has an aggression problem, don't ignore it. Don't ignore the warning signals, and don't make excuses. Without help, it will probably get worse. Dogs learn that biting works; it drives away the source of their stress. Once a dog bites, he is more likely to bite again.

There are legal concerns in owning an aggressive dog. Society is increasingly intolerant of any nuisance created by dogs, and dog bites in particular are receiving a lot of publicity. New laws are being passed that emphasize the owner's liability for his dog's actions.

But more important than the legal concerns are the moral concerns. No one should have to suffer the pain and emotional trauma of a dog bite or attack. The emotional and physical effects can last a lifetime. Since dogs are everywhere in our society, a fear of dogs created by an attack can be a real handicap.

As emphasized at the beginning of this chapter, seek professional help from someone with experience in aggression who utilizes positive reinforcement training.

The author's Irish Setter drives through the weave poles in agility competition.

10

Great Adventures with Your Dog

There are many fun things you can do with your dog, especially once he has some basic training. This chapter will give you some suggestions. Besides being fun, the activities in this chapter provide your dog with the mental stimulation he needs to be happy. Dogs need more than physical exercise. They need mental exercise, too. They are intelligent, thinking beings who enjoy new experiences. And not only your dog will get mental stimulation. You will learn a lot, too.

Dog activities also provide a unique opportunity to meet new people. There is something about dogs that makes it easy to start a conversation with a stranger. Maybe it is because you don't have to start off by talking about yourself or the other person. The furry bodies on the end of the leash are easy to talk about. So read on. See if there is anything that might interest you and your dog. You both could use something new to do, couldn't you?

Obedience Classes

Even after you have successfully completed the training detailed in this book, you can still benefit from attending a good obedience class. Training in a class gives you the opportunity to train around the distractions of a room full of dogs and people. It provides your dog with exposure to a different place as well as socialization with dogs and strange people. A good instructor can help you learn how to read your dog. He or she can tell you when your dog is confused and when he is refusing to obey.

Finding a good class can be difficult. If you can't find a good one, don't go at all. Some classes are taught in such a violent manner that they can do damage to your dog and your relationship. Obedience classes are taught by all sorts of groups and individuals. It is important to know that dog trainers are not licensed in any way. Anyone can declare himself a dog trainer, so you have to be very careful. Some correspondence schools declare people dog trainers who have just read about dog training and observed one class. One person apprenticed with me, and when I told her she wasn't ready yet to teach classes, she left and opened her own school.

Classes can be offered by private individuals, privately owned training schools, boarding kennels, recreation departments, community colleges, kennel clubs, obedience clubs, or the adult education programs of your local school district. Any of these classes can be good or bad. The best classes are often not widely advertised because they are easily filled by word of mouth. Ask your friends who own dogs and your veterinarian for referrals.

In choosing an obedience class instructor, be sure not to equate dog training success with ability to instruct a class. These are related but different skills. A person may be able to train his dog to high honors in obedience competitions but be unable to teach someone else how to do it. Being able to teach people is different from being able to teach dogs, and both skills are needed to be a good dog obedience instructor. There is one national organization that does endorse obedience instructors. It is the National Association of Dog Obedience Instructors (NADOI). An instructor becomes a member of NADOI, which constitutes endorsement, by having at least a few years of experience teaching and by taking an extensive written test. Membership in NADOI at least indicates that an instructor is experienced and is interested enough in his profession to support such an organization. However, not all NADOI instructors may be to your liking, and there are many good obedience instructors who do not have NADOI endorsement. You can contact NADOI at nadoi.org. Another national organization of obedience instructors is the Association of Pet Dog Trainers (APDT). While they do not test trainers, they do have a list of trainers on their Web site at apdt.com. Keep in mind that not all of the trainers belonging to these organizations use positive reinforcement training.

Please don't take your dog to a kennel and leave him there to be trained. This type of training is often much more expensive but less successful. The trainer may be able to give you an impressive demonstration at the end of the training, but your dog is not going to continue living at the kennel, and the trainer won't be coming home with you to keep up the training. Even if you are given a lesson in how to handle your dog at the end of this type of training, one or two lessons is not enough to learn what to do if your dog does not respond to your commands. You will have missed the benefits of learning to read your dog as you train him, as well as the benefits of the strong bond that develops between a dog and his trainer. Worse still, this

A Cavalier King Charles Spaniel flies over an agility jump.

kind of training can be abusive. You have no control over what is done to your dog in your absence.

Don't attend a class without finding out some information first. The best thing to do is to observe a class before you sign up. If an instructor or training organization won't let you do this, eliminate it from your list. What do you look for? First of all, do the dogs and owners look stressed, unhappy, or intimidated? Unless the dogs are shy, they should not be scared. Is the instructor clear in his instructions to the class? Remember, an obedience class instructor is teaching people, not training dogs. Does the instructor give the students a lot of positive reinforcement, pointing out when they do something well, or does he just yell when they do something wrong? He should be friendly and willing to talk to students before or after class. A sense of humor can be a real asset. Obedience classes do not need to be unpleasant to be effective. In fact, you will be more likely to complete the class if it is fun.

Observing a class prior to signing up is not always possible. If not, you have to ask a lot of questions. Here is a good list to go through:

1. Is the class size limited? I think 8 to 10 is an ideal number. If there are more, ask if there is an assistant instructor to help out. Obviously, the more people in a class, the less personal attention you will receive.

2. What is the instructor's experience? How did he learn to teach classes? Did he have some sort of apprenticeship? How long has he been teaching dog obedience classes? Of course, experience doesn't

necessarily make someone good. In fact, someone who has taught for 20 years may be teaching by out-of-date methods. A good instructor tries to improve himself by reading books and dog training magazines and by attending training seminars.

3. Does the instructor use food rewards? If you agree with the ideas presented in this book, you may be uncomfortable with not using food and relying more on force. However, there are many different yet successful ways to train a dog. If the instructor doesn't allow the use of food in his class, make more effort to observe a class before signing up. Keep in mind that you can refuse to follow an instructor's directions if you feel something may be detrimental to your dog.

4. What is taught in the class? Does the instruction concentrate on practical training you can use every day, or is training for showing emphasized?

Of course, you will want to ask about the price and length of the class. An average class length is 8 to 12 weeks, with the class meeting one hour per week. Are there homework sheets to help you with your practice at home? What equipment does the instructor prefer you to use? Does the instructor sound flexible in his training methods? Beware of any instructor who says there is only one way to train all dogs. Dogs and people are too different for one method to be effective for everyone.

Obedience classes are a good way to spend quality time with your dog. They will provide you with motivation to practice every week, if only because you won't want to look foolish at the next class. You and your dog will make new friends. If you find a good class, it can be lots of fun for both of you. Do it!

Joining a Dog Club

A good way to get involved in activities with your dog, meet a wide variety of people, and further your knowledge about dogs is to join a dog club. Most clubs are affiliated with the American Kennel Club and are involved in holding shows and matches. There are at least a few in every state, but sometimes these clubs can be difficult to locate. Because they are nonprofit organizations run by volunteers, most cannot afford a listing in the phone book. A list of AKC dog clubs is available on the AKC's Web site at akc.org. Not all dog clubs are affiliated with the AKC, however. Check with other dog lovers or your veterinarian to find other dog clubs in your area.

Dog clubs vary in their character and their activities. AKC clubs can be all-breed clubs that may or may not include obedience training in their activities, or they may be obedience clubs. Clubs that are devoted to a single breed are called specialty clubs. Other AKC clubs have their main interest in hunting dogs. As with any organization, some clubs are more welcoming to new members than others. All these clubs will be involved in putting on dog shows, matches, field trials, or hunting tests. In addition, they will probably have a variety of other activities. They may have monthly meetings that feature guest speakers or videotapes on dogs. They will probably have some social events, such as a Christmas party. Many AKC clubs hold handling or obedience classes. Some clubs give demonstrations at local shopping malls or county fairs, while others may sponsor seminars given by experts on some aspect of dogs.

A favorite activity of the club I belong to is visiting nursing homes with our dogs. There are clubs that specialize in this. We give a brief obedience demonstration, then do something fun, like playing musical chairs or square dancing with our dogs. After our program, we walk the dogs around to visit the residents, who pet the dogs and often share stories of a dog they have owned in the past. The activities directors of the nursing homes tell us that these are the most popular programs of the year. The dogs (and their owners!) love showing off. Everyone gets something out of it, not the least of which is our sense of self-satisfaction.

Whenever I have moved, one of the first things I have done is contact the local dog club. It has always been a great way to make new friends. The diversity of people who belong to dog clubs is fascinating. Through dog clubs, my dogs have been able to participate in a variety of activities that provide them with the mental stimulation they need. Besides joining in club activities, I have always managed to find someone who shares my love for hiking with the dogs. The people I have met have greatly enriched my life. Maybe joining a dog club can do that for you, too!

Showing Your Dog

Dog shows, whether breed, obedience, agility, or many dog sports, are the most popular meeting ground of dog lovers. Some shows have more than 3,000 entries. They provide an opportunity to learn more about dogs, make new friends, and travel. They also provide an opportunity to get up at ridiculously early hours in the morning, drive many miles, spend hours outdoors in bad weather, and eat bad food, all in the pursuit of a ribbon. It's a funny game, played with a dog for a partner.

Many titles, such as obedience and agility titles, can be attained without having to win over other dogs, leading to a special camaraderie with others who participate. Everyone cheers for everyone else. Showing dogs has led me to lifelong friendships that I treasure. Best of all, showing dogs gives me goals that challenge me to perfect my communication with my dog.

Showing your dog can be an experience that is beneficial to your relationship with your dog, but it can also be detrimental. It is wonderful to travel with your dog to shows, sharing quality time together and the challenge of showing. On the other hand, the lust for wins and the ego gratification they bring can sometimes lead owners to neglect their dogs' needs. The search for a winning show dog can result in an accumulation of dogs, whereby you can find yourself giving up the quality of human-dog relationship. It is important to keep in mind that dog shows satisfy people's needs, not dogs'.

Showing in Obedience

Training a dog to show in obedience is a great way to build a very special relationship with your dog. The purpose of obedience competition, as stated in the AKC's obedience regulations, is "to demonstrate the usefulness of the purebred dog as a companion to man." In obedience competition, dogs are judged on performance only. Appearance does not count. There are three levels of competition: Novice, Open, and Utility. Obedience titles are obtained by achieving three qualifying scores at each level. A dog who is spayed or neutered can compete, as they can in other dog sports, like agility and hunting tests. AKC obedience competition is only available to purebred AKC dogs, but mixed breeds can compete in UKC obedience. A dog who appears to be purebred but doesn't have AKC papers can get a special number

The high jump is a part of advanced obedience competition. (Border Collie)

AKC Obedience Competition Exercises

Exercise	Description of Exericise
Novice	
Heel on Leash and Figure 8	Includes sitting at halt, about turns, changes of speed
Stand for Examination	Done off leash; exam done by judge, handler six feet away
Heel Off Leash	Same as heel on leash, but performed off leash
Recall	Come when called from a sit-stay, 35 feet away
Sit Stay	Off leash, handler 30 feet away, one minute, with group of dogs
Down-Stay	Same as above, except three minutes
Open	
Heel Off Leash and Figure 8	Same as in Novice
Drop on Recall	Dog must stop and lie down while coming
Retrieve	Dog stays while dumbbell thrown, then retrieves and sits
Retrieve Over High Jump	Jump height equals the dog's shoulder height
Broad Jump	A long jump twice the distance of the high jump
Sit–Stay, Out of Sight	Done for three minutes with handler out of dog's sight
Down-Stay, Out of Sight	Done for five minutes with handler out of dog's sight
Utility	
Signal Exercise	Dog stands, stays, lies down, sits, and comes with hand signals only
Scent Discrimination	Dog finds object with handler's scent on it
Directed Retrieve	Dog retrieves one of three gloves
Moving Stand and Exam	Dog stays in stand while handler keeps moving; judge does exam
Directed Jumping	Dog runs away from handler for 40 feet, sits and jumps as directed

called an ILP number in order to compete. Copies of the obedience regulations are available free of charge from the AKC at their Web site at akc.org.

The easiest way to get started showing your dog is to take a class to learn how to do it. There are two types of classes, one for each of the two types of showing: obedience classes and handling classes, which teach you how to show in breed. As mentioned above, joining a dog club is a good way to get started showing dogs. Members can share their knowledge with you. Also enjoying the company and support of club members at shows makes the shows much more enjoyable.

If you cannot find classes, there are great videos on obedience training. A wealth of information is available by simply going to a show and watching. Once you feel you are ready to give it a try, the place to start is at a match. This is a practice show available for both breed and obedience showing. More about this below.

Showing in Breed

Breed, or conformation, shows are the beauty shows of dogs. They are the kind of show you've seen on TV every February at the Westminster Kennel Club. These shows actually have the serious purpose of maintaining the appearance and healthy structure of purebred dogs so it is known which dogs are the ones most deserving of being bred. Judges aren't picking the prettiest dog. They are judging the dogs against the nationally accepted description of the breed, called a standard. Judges feel the dog's bone structure and watch the dogs trot to assess their ability to move. Dogs earn championships by earning points. These points are earned by defeating other dogs in competition. Once a dog earns 15 points, he is awarded a championship for a lifetime.

Dogs are shown in good physical condition with beautiful, skillfully groomed coats. While it may look easy, showing in the breed ring is quite an art. Some people hire professional handlers to groom and show their dogs.

Before you invest much time and money in showing a dog in breed, it is a good idea to find out if your dog is of good enough quality to be competitive. Just because your dog is AKC registered does not mean he is show quality. Very few are. Your chances are best if one or both of your dog's parents have their championships. Try to have your dog evaluated by someone you trust who is knowledgeable about your breed. This could be someone who has finished a few championships on dogs of your breed, or it could be someone who handles dogs in the showring professionally. A good place to learn more about your dog's quality is to purchase the AKC video about your particular breed from the AKC. There are handling classes to learn how to show your dog in breed, and matches are the place to get started.

Showing a Whippet in breed (or conformation) competition.

Matches

Matches are practice dog shows. Their purpose is to give a person or dog new to the sport of dog showing an opportunity to practice before entering licensed dog shows. Matches are smaller than regular dog shows, more informal, and less expensive, and can usually be entered the same day instead of several weeks ahead of time, as is required for regular shows.

Matches can offer breed, obedience, or both. Agility matches are also held. In breed matches, puppies can start as young as three months old. Matches may or may not be AKC sanctioned. Those not AKC sanctioned are often called *fun matches* or *show and go's* and allow mixed breeds.

Matches also provide a training ground for judges. Keep this in mind when you enter one. Your dog may be scored differently in obedience or placed differently in breed by a more experienced judge at a regular show.

Irish Setter enjoying agility competition.

Canine Good Citizen Test

In 1989 the AKC introduced the Canine Good Citizen program. It is open to mixed breed as well as purebred dogs. The purpose of the test is to demonstrate that a dog has good manners. It is noncompetitive. Handlers may talk to their dogs and give extra commands. A certificate will be sent from the AKC for all dogs that pass. A dog must pass all 10 parts of the test to earn a certificate. All parts are performed on leash. The 10 parts are:

1. *Accepting a Friendly Stranger.* Tester and owner will shake hands.
2. *Sitting Politely for Petting.* Dog sits to be petted by tester.
3. *Appearance and Grooming.* Tester brushes dog, handles his ears and paws.
4. *Walking on a Loose Leash.* Dog does turns and halts. He does not need to heel.
5. *Walking Through a Crowd.* Dogs walks around people without jumping on them.
6. *Sit and Down on Command/Staying in Place.* Dog sits and lies down. Then handler walks away 20 feet and returns. The dog is on a 20-foot line.
7. *Coming When Called.* Dog is on a long line and comes 10 feet.
8. *Reaction to Another Dog.* Two handlers and dogs approach each other, stop and shake hands.

9. *Reactions to Distractions.* Distractions may be a jogger passing by and a loud noise.

10. *Supervised Separation.* Someone will hold your dog while you go out of sight for three minutes.

Rally and Rally-O

Rally is another obedience sport, but one that puts less emphasis on precision and more on enjoyment. Rally is an AKC sport; Rally-O is open to all dogs, including mixed breeds. In both, handler and dog complete a course involving mostly heeling. A sequence of signs is set up that tells the handler what to do. The big difference is that you can talk to and praise your dog while working. In the beginning levels of Rally-O, treats can be used. Rally obedience is a fun way to prepare for competitive obedience and is a good way to provide attention to older dogs. More information on Rally and Rally-O is available at apdt.com.

Agility

Agility is an exciting and fun dog activity involving an obstacle course for dogs. You may have seen it on TV. Agility courses consist of about 13 to 20 obstacles. These include jumps, tunnels, A-frames for climbing, a raised dog walk, tires to jump through, and weave poles. Jump heights are adjusted to the height of the dog, so every size dog can compete.

A Lhasa Apso scales the peak of the A-frame, an obstacle used in agility.

Golden Retriever on the A-frame in agility competition.

The AKC is the main organization offering agility competitions in the United States, but there are others like USDAA, NADAC, and UKC that allow mixed breeds to compete.

If you have a chance to try agility, don't pass it up. Even if you don't plan to compete, it is a great confidence builder for dogs and a fun way to practice stay and off-leash obedience. It's best to take a basic obedience class first before trying an agility class. Introductory classes are mostly taught on leash. There's nothing better for your relationship with your dog than having fun together.

Therapy Dogs

A great way to share your trained dog is doing therapy dog work. Whether you go by yourself or as part of a group, you'll find yourself welcome at most nursing homes. My dog club goes as a group to several local nursing homes. We perform a little obedience and a lot of tricks for the residents, then visit with each resident individually for petting time. Residents love to talk about their past dogs. Other ways you can do therapy dog work with your dog is with hospital patients, particularly those in rehabilitation, or with families in shelters. My Irish Setter and I enjoy participating in a huge local Christmas party for disadvantaged children with my dog club. We entertain the children while they are waiting in line. Kyra must have jumped through her hula hoop a hundred times! We both loved it.

There are organizations that certify dogs as therapy dogs. These include Therapy Dogs International, Therapy Dogs, Inc., and Delta Society Pet Partners. Some of the tests resemble the AKC Canine Good Citizen test. As always, get started with basic obedience training, the foundation for all dog activities.

Patients will love the company and having a soft, warm body to pet. Your dog will love the attention, and you will feel good about helping someone less fortunate. Everybody wins!

Special Activities for Special Breeds

Lure coursing, herding tests, and AKC hunting tests are all examples of dog sports that are based on the job for which breeds were developed. Earthdog tests allow small terriers and Dachshunds the opportunity to find rats in a cage underground. Man's competitive nature led to the design of ways to test these skills. Such tests are also a means to identify and measure these instinctive behaviors so they can be preserved in breeding programs, since most dogs no longer have the opportunity to engage in the work for which they were bred. Because these dog sports utilize the instincts of the dogs, the dogs love them. They are a fun and challenging way for you and your dog to spend time together. If you own one of the breeds used in these sports, try to go see such an event. Like dog showing, if kept in the proper prospective, they provide a fascinating hobby and an opportunity to make new friends. Giving your dog the opportunity to make use of his instinctive behavior will make him happier, and it is a great way to continue building your relationship with your dog.

Lure Coursing

Lure coursing is a modern version of a sport that has been practiced since ancient times. Coursing on live game is illegal in most places, so an artificial lure is now used. This is done by dragging a white plastic bag at fast speeds along the ground in a pattern full of irregular turns in an open field. The breeds allowed to compete are Afghans, Basenjis, Borzois, Greyhounds, Ibizen Hounds, Irish Wolfhounds, Pharaoh Hounds, Salukis, Scottish Deerhounds, and Whippets. These breeds are called sighthounds because they hunt by sight.

Lure coursing relies on the dog's instinct to chase a moving object, and little training is required, other than making sure a dog is in adequate physical condition. Usually three dogs run at a time. It is beautiful and inspiring to watch. Most sighthounds love it, and it gives them an opportunity to exercise. As mentioned above, lure coursing also enables breeders to evaluate their stock to choose suitable animals for breeding. Practice runs are often available for a small cost after licensed trials.

These Borzoi are being released at the start of a lure course.

Lure coursing is not judged on speed alone. Rather, the dogs receive scores for agility, following the lure, enthusiasm, endurance, and speed. Winners receive ribbons. Points are awarded based on how many dogs are beaten at each course, with 100 points being required to attain a field championship.

Note that this is different from Greyhound racing. First of all, it is open to more breeds. The courses are not run on a track, but in an open field. The dogs involved in lure coursing are people's pets, not part of a racing industry. There is no gambling involved in this sport.

A Whippet pushes off to a good start.

Lure coursing trials are part of the American Kennel Club's performance dog sports. The American Sighthound Field Association (ASFA) also holds trials.

Herding Tests

Herding is an aspect of canine hunting behavior that man has made good use of. Various hunting behaviors present in our dogs' wolflike ancestors were selectively bred over many generations to produce dogs exhibiting special abilities, such as sighthounds and herding dogs.

The AKC offers a set of herding tests for all of the AKC herding breeds, such as German Shepherds, Border Collies, and Corgis, plus Samoyeds and Rottweilers. In herding sports, dogs move sheep, and sometimes ducks and cattle, as if they were on a farm. There are two types of tests: Herding Tests, which are noncompetitive and require less training, and Herding Trials, which are competitive. Herding Tests allow a dog to demonstrate instincts toward herding. Stock use can be sheep, ducks, or cattle. In Herding Trials, dogs must show their ability to herd under the directions of a person. Border Collies who are AKC registered can compete in AKC herding trials, but Border Collies also have their own competition organization, the U.S. Border Collie Handlers Association. Contact them at usbcha.com.

AKC Hunting Tests

Do you want to see if your Golden Retriever, Irish Setter, or Springer Spaniel still has the hunting instincts for which his breed was developed?

This Belgian Tervuren is learning to herd sheep.

Giving the direction for a retrieve is part of the AKC retriever hunting test. (Golden Retriever)

Then the AKC's hunting tests are for you. Hunting tests got their start when the first test was held in 1985 as a noncompetitive alternative to field trials. Field trials are expensive and time-consuming, certainly beyond the reach of the average dog owner. For instance, pointing breed field trials require that the dogs be handled from horseback. In contrast, handlers walk in the hunting tests for the same breeds.

    The hunting tests are divided into tests for retrievers, pointers, and spaniels. There are three levels of difficulty. After qualifying a specified number of times, your dog is awarded the titles of junior hunter, senior hunter, or the most difficult, master hunter.

As an example, let's look at the requirements for the junior hunter retriever test. The retriever must do a minimum of four retrieves, two on land and two on water. Distances should not exceed 100 yards. The dog must retrieve to hand, not dropping the bird or refusing to give it up. Live ducks are used and shot. Dogs are scored on marking (memory of where the bird has fallen), style, nose (scenting ability), perseverance, and trainability. The tests should imitate natural hunting conditions as much as possible.

These tests are rapidly increasing in popularity. If you want to see one, contact the AKC for help in finding the one nearest you.

Fun and Fitness with Your Dog

Most dogs love to be outdoors and active. Finding ways to indulge your dog in these pleasures may introduce you to new activities and new ways of enjoying old ones.

What do you do if you live in Vermont, where snow covers the ground for many months, and you have to exercise two big dogs? When I was in that position, I learned to cross-country ski, which proved to be great exercise for me and my dogs. The dogs had to learn to stay out of the way of swinging ski poles, heel with a skier, and get off the trail when snowmobiles approached. Mine had to learn that when I fell, it was not an invitation to play. One of the hardest things to teach them, and something that was the cause of a few spectacular crashes until they learned, was that when they were running in front of us on a downhill section and we yelled their names, we did *not* want them to stop and turn around to look at us!

In the summer, when it is too hot for your dog to exercise any other way, swimming is the activity of choice. You will probably have to get into the water with him to build his confidence about stepping off into water that is over his head. Support him under his belly while he gets the feel of it. Don't count on your dog being able to swim instinctively. I have seen dogs jump into the water and let themselves sink without making any effort to save themselves. Dogs may also flail around with their front legs and try to climb out of the water, spinning in circles and going nowhere. It helps if your dog can play with another dog who loves to swim. If he likes to retrieve, you might be able to entice him into swimming by throwing something just a little farther each time until he is forced to swim. You can introduce puppies as young as eight weeks old to the water. It takes a little longer for an adult dog to relax in the water, but most can learn to love it. Swimming is the perfect exercise for older dogs with arthritis.

Hiking is a great activity to share with a dog. This may take the form of a two-hour walk in the woods, or an overnight expedition. I live along the Appalachian Trail, and I meet dogs who are hiking with their owners all

Cross-country skiing is a good way to enjoy the snow with your dog. (Belgian Tervuren)

the way from Georgia to Maine. A good combination is hiking with a dog play group. It is so relaxing to walk and talk with good friends, while the dogs play with each other.

There are other ways to share the outdoors with your dog. We've already discussed jogging with your dog in the chapter on exercising your dog. You could take your dog with you on horseback rides or let him gather all the tennis balls you hit over the fence. We enjoy canoeing with our dogs. Believe it or not, they quickly learn to balance. A good response to the "stay" command is a necessity when they want to jump out to chase a duck! Whatever you do, dogs (*trained* dogs, that is) and the outdoors are a natural combination.

To Breed or Not to Breed

When talking about things to do with your dog, breeding your dog is something that might come to mind. Bringing new lives into the world is a responsibility that should not be taken lightly, especially in a world where millions of unwanted dogs are killed every year.

There are different kinds of breeders. Good breeders strive to breed the healthiest, most beautiful dogs with the best temperaments possible. They show their dogs to get an objective opinion about the quality of their dogs. They are knowledgeable about the genetic diseases of their breed and have had their dogs tested to reduce the possibility of passing these genes on. These puppies come with a health and temperament guarantee.

Good breeders are also very selective about the homes in which they place their puppies. They will interview prospective buyers extensively. If they cannot find the right homes, they are prepared to keep the puppies until they do. They put great effort into educating their puppy buyers about how to raise and care for their dog. If for any reason you cannot keep your dog, good breeders want to know about it because they feel responsible for each and every puppy they have produced. If there is any way they can, they will take the dog back, at any age. Their passion for their breed is evident when you speak to them.

There are also what is commonly referred to as "backyard" breeders. These are people with no real knowledge of the breed. They just think their dog is nice and that it would be fun to have puppies. Besides, they might be able to make some money. After all, they paid enough for their dog. These casual breeders' choice of stud is based on convenience rather than quality; they use any dog of the same breed who happens to live close by. They have probably heard of hip dysplasia but don't really know what it is. Their dog seems fine, so they are not worried about the disease. They don't know that their dog is too young to show any signs of the hereditary disease unless she was X-rayed. Their knowledge of how to housebreak and train a puppy is limited, so they won't be able to give you any advice. This kind of breeder doesn't really care anyway. That's the buyer's problem. As long as you have the money, the puppy is yours.

What kind of breeder would you rather buy a puppy from? What kind of breeder do you want to be? If you can't be a good breeder, you shouldn't be a breeder at all.

If you want to be a good breeder, the first question you should ask yourself is whether your dog is of good enough quality to breed. Just because your

Many dogs love to go swimming. (Golden Retriever)

dog is a nice family pet with AKC papers is not reason enough. Because there are a limited number of good homes available, only the best dogs should be bred. Your dog should have a perfect temperament, be a good specimen of his or her breed, and be free of all hereditary diseases. Hereditary diseases are abundant in purebred dogs. Just because your dog seems healthy does not mean he doesn't have such diseases as hip dysplasia or cataracts. *You don't know if you haven't had him checked.* It is irresponsible to breed a dog without a thorough check for all hereditary diseases known to occur in the breed.

Be honest with yourself in assessing your dog's temperament. Don't make excuses for your dog's shy or aggressive personality. There is no way to know for certain if the problem is hereditary or not, so don't take the chance of breeding more puppies with a similar problem. Also consider your dog's trainability in evaluating his temperament.

The second thing you should ask yourself is if you have the qualities and knowledge necessary to be a good breeder. Do you know the signs that your dog is having difficulty delivering a puppy and is in need of immediate veterinary attention? Do you know what to do if a puppy doesn't start breathing when delivered? Do you know how to choose a stud? Do you know what your state laws are regarding the sale of puppies?

Do you have the time? Several things can cause a mother dog to be unable to nurse her puppies, such as mastitis (an infection of the breasts). In such cases, you will need to feed the puppies often and around the clock. Even after they are weaned, you will have to be there four times a day to feed them. You will also spend a lot of time cleaning up after them. If your life is already hectic, do you really have the time?

Then there is the problem of placing the puppies. Do you feel you can adequately screen buyers to prevent your puppy from being placed in a home where he will not be properly cared for? For instance, what are your feelings about placing a puppy in a home without a fenced yard? Are you sure there is a demand for puppies of your breed? If your breed is popular, there may not only be a demand for puppies, but there may also be a flood of them advertised in the newspaper. What are you going to do if you cannot find homes for the puppies?

You can be responsible for a tremendous amount of dog suffering if you do not carefully interview and screen your buyers. An all-too-common story is a puppy who is left alone all day without being confined while his owners work. When the owners return home to find their furniture ripped to shreds and messes all over the floor, they beat the dog and chain him up in the backyard. The dog suffers at the end of the chain, receiving inadequate care and no love, until he is abandoned at the local animal shelter and mercifully euthanized. Don't kid yourself. This happens to purebred dogs as well as to mixed breeds.

A Belgian Tervuren is flying off the box that shoots out tennis balls for flyball competitions.

Think about the millions of unwanted dogs who are killed annually. Is it really necessary for you to breed your dog?

Conclusion

All the activities mentioned here are growing in popularity. They are actually just a sampling of the many activities available to dog owners. Flyball, water rescue tests, and cart pulling are just a few of many more. All this reflects the growing interest people have in doing things with their dogs. The AKC has responded to these new demands by adding several activities that evaluate how dogs perform, rather than just how they look. These changes also reflect a growing appreciation for a dog's intelligence and respect for his abilities.

If you aren't interested in pursuing any of these activities with your dog, please remember his need for mental stimulation. Include him in family activities as much as possible. Take him places with you, on errands or to the kids' soccer games. Try taking your dog with you when you travel. The inconveniences involved will be compensated for by the interesting experiences you will have.

What you get out of your relationship with your dog is proportional to what you put into it. Anything you do to spend quality time with your dog will improve your relationship, but facing new challenges and learning together will give your relationship a unique depth. The rewards are worth it.

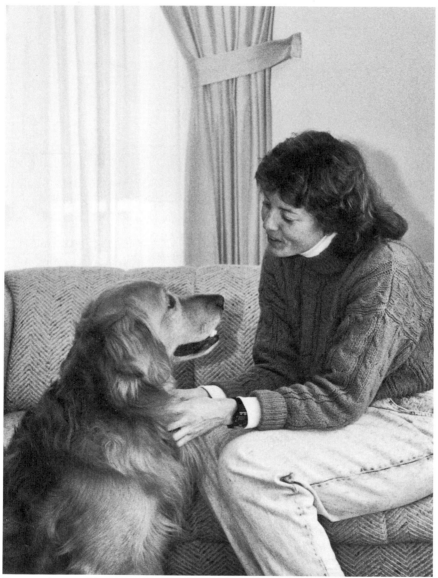

Dogs make good listeners. (Golden Retriever)

11

Lessons to Learn from Our Dogs

There are lessons you can learn from your dog and the process of training him that have wider application than just to dog training. What you have learned in training your dog can be applied in your relationships with humans. Developing a good relationship, be it with a dog or with another person, involves similar skills.

Dogs offer good examples for us. Everyone who owns a dog knows how pleasing it is to be greeted by their dog when they return home. Their dog doesn't complain about what happened to him during the day, he isn't mad about a fight from the night before, and he doesn't make any immediate demands. He is just happy to see you. Wouldn't you like to be greeted that way by everyone? Try it yourself. Greet someone, like your husband or wife, when he or she gets home from work, or your kids when they get home from school, the same way your dog greets you. No, I don't mean wagging your tail or jumping up on them. I mean meeting them at the door with a smile, acting happy to see them, and listening, refraining from complaints or demands.

By learning from our dogs about building a good relationship and the power of positive reinforcement, about the importance of nonverbal communication and who we are, and most of all about love, we may finally become as noble as our dogs think we are.

Building a Good Relationship

Patience, good listening skills, empathy, tolerance, and realistic expectations—these are all skills that make for a good relationship, whether it is with a dog or a person.

In the first chapter and throughout this book, realistic expectations regarding your dog have been emphasized. Whenever your expectations of your dog are not fulfilled, your disappointment and frustration can lead you to dislike your dog. The same is true of human relationships. When a person doesn't live up to someone else's expectations, serious problems develop in the relationship. False expectations can lead you to think that the person or dog is purposely acting in a way to hurt you. The relationship then becomes one of adversaries. The adversarial relationship people develop with their dogs reminds me of the adversarial relationships people have with one another. It may be between marriage partners, between parent and child, or with anybody. Fighting develops. Dogs are punished; people hurt each other. It is impossible to build a good relationship without realistic expectations.

Tolerance is based on realistic expectations. You have to develop a lot of tolerance to live with a dog. He has different needs and priorities. For example, keeping your house clean is not as important to your dog as it is to you. When you own a dog, you have to learn to tolerate having dirt tracked in and hair shedding. Your dog has shown you that in order for him to meet your need for a well-behaved dog, you have to meet his need for exercise. This understanding of needs and priorities is essential for good human relationships, too.

Wrong assumptions regarding the meaning of another's behavior are destructive to good relationships. When you return home to find that your dog has destroyed something in your absence, it is tempting to think that he has done this out of spite. As was discussed in chapter 8, this isn't true; usually destructive chewing is done out of fear of being left alone. Assuming your dog chewed on the woodwork because he resents being left alone is a reflection of feeling guilty about leaving a dog alone. These wrong assumptions can lead to harming your relationship with your dog by inappropriate punishment.

The same thing can happen with wrong assumptions in human relationships. Take, for example, a child who is caught stealing. The parents assume that the child is simply greedy and wants more than he has. The child is punished. However, the real reason for the stealing may have been that the child craves the parents' attention and thinks this is the only way of getting it. The solution to the real problem is more than punishment.

Good communication is the foundation of all good relationships, and listening is the foundation of good communication. Most people talk to their dogs, not because their dogs can understand them, and not because they think their dog is going to offer good advice, but because dogs are such good listeners. They can't talk back, they can't interrupt you, and they can't argue with you. They give you their full attention.

Mutual good listening is true of good dog training and good friendships. You have to "listen" to your dog's body language to train him well. You also have to train him to listen to you. I am fascinated by the similarities between the techniques used to train dogs for obedience competition to ensure they aren't distracted in the ring while performing, and the listening skills taught in marriage improvement seminars. All your relationships would be better if you learned to listen as well as your dog does.

Many people find it easier to develop a good relationship with a dog than with another person. Dogs can't talk back and aren't as judgmental. Training your dog can give you the insight necessary to apply these skills to other areas of your life.

The Power of Positive Reinforcement

The most important lesson you can learn from training your dog with the techniques described in this book is the power of positive reinforcement. People respond to positive reinforcement just as well as dogs do.

One reason my obedience classes are successful is that I pay special attention to positively reinforcing the owners. I don't use food, of course; praise is a good reward for people. In a class of beginners, it would be easy to constantly find fault with their performance and only point out what they are doing wrong, but that would be discouraging and would lead to people dropping out of the class. Rather, I make a point of praising the owners. Even with the worst-behaved dog in class, I manage to find some small improvement to praise. The owners feel good about their accomplishments, so they keep practicing, in spite of the many frustrations involved in training. The owners are eventually rewarded with a trained dog.

You can integrate positive reinforcement into many aspects of your life. When my husband wanted to increase the number of patients he saw in a day, he pushed his staff to speed up and become more efficient. It didn't work. Then I suggested trying positive reinforcement. He offered a bonus if a certain goal was met. This time, productivity increased, and everyone was happier. Making positive reinforcement part of your life is as simple as putting more energy in saying thank you and rewarding people when they do something you like, and less in complaining when they do something wrong.

All the disadvantages of punishing a dog apply to humans, too. Just as in dogs, punishment can create fear, avoidance, resentment, and secretiveness. It cuts off communication, and it doesn't teach what you want. Look how ineffective prison is as a punishment for criminals.

Punishment is as destructive to human relationships as it is to dogs. A common reaction of a wife to a husband who frequently comes home late from work is to criticize him and start a fight; she is punishing him. The husband, dreading the scene when he comes home from work, avoids the situation by coming home later and later. A better tactic for the wife would be to ignore the late arrivals and reward him when he comes home on time. At first, he may even have to be rewarded for coming home a little less late. The reward could be meeting him at the door in a good mood, listening sympathetically to his complaints about work, and getting him something to drink. He may be more anxious to come home on time in the future. While punishment works in some situations, it must be balanced by positive reinforcement to maintain a good relationship.

It is hard to break the habit of punishment. It is the method most people choose to deal with problem behavior, whether it is a person or a dog who is misbehaving. I often have trouble convincing people to stop punishing their dogs, even though they admit that the punishment is not working. Punishment is part of our culture. It provides a release for anger and a means to dominate and control. The world would be a better place if the urge to punish and control was replaced by the urge to understand and help.

Positive reinforcement works as well for my obedience students as for their dogs. (Rhodesian Ridgeback)

The Importance of Nonverbal Communication

Dogs always seem so honest and sensitive—qualities we would like to have in ourselves and in the people around us. That dogs have these qualities is related to the fact that they communicate nonverbally. They seem honest because, without being able to talk, they cannot lie.

Dogs seem sensitive because they read our body language. They are good at it because this is the way they communicate with each other. Dogs cannot be misled by the things we say. We cannot hide our feelings from them with words. For instance, when someone asks you how you are, you may respond by saying you are fine, even when you are not. The person to whom you are speaking may miss the nonverbal messages that say you are not fine, such as slumped body posture and a depressed tone of voice if you are sad, or tense body posture and an abrupt tone of voice if you are angry. Your dog would never make this mistake, and neither should you when you are communicating with other people or you will miss an important part of their message. If you ask someone what's wrong, and they reply, "Nothing," but their body language says something else, don't ignore the real message. Reading and responding to body language improve communication; this, in turn, improves relationships.

Dogs Are Our Mirrors

Often the first awareness I have of being in a particular mood is when it is reflected in my dog. Her behavior reflects my tension or my relaxation, my anxiety or my peacefulness, my depression or my happiness. When I am in a bad mood, I often find her hiding in her crate, avoiding me. Seeing this makes me feel terrible. I can then put things in perspective and relax, much to the relief of the rest of my family. My dog, acting as a mirror, has helped me to see myself.

Dogs act as mirrors in many ways. Our choice of dogs tells us something about ourselves. Why is it that some people choose to rescue dogs from Humane Societies, while others choose to buy expensive, purebred dogs? And what about your choice of breed? My past choices of a Borzoi and a Greyhound as pets reflected my desire to project to the world an image of elegance and sophistication. My current choice of an Irish Setter mirrors my desire to have more fun and lightheartedness in my own life. My husband, on the other hand, chooses a Belgian Tervuren, a breed that is not readily recognized and, in fact, is often mistaken for a Collie/Shepherd mix. This reflects his distaste for displays of wealth (besides his smart choice of a more trainable breed). Both of our choices of unusual breeds reveal a mutual desire to be seen as a little different from other people.

A dog's sensitivity makes him a wonderful mirror of your moods. The way you have raised and trained him also reveals something about yourself.

Training your dog magnifies the mirror effect because your relationship is intensified by the communication effort. Are you apt to lose your temper with your dog, or are you quick to blame him when he doesn't understand what you want? When you become frustrated, do you give up, or do you tend to resort to physical force? Are you afraid that if you are assertive in your training efforts your dog will not love you? What does the way you train your dog tell you about yourself?

As an obedience instructor, I see many examples of the mirror effect. For instance, there is always a strong correlation between well-behaved dogs and well-behaved children. The dog who cannot concentrate and is easily distracted is a clear reflection of his owner, who arrives late to class, has forgotten her dog's training collar, and misses half the instructions because she is talking to someone else. The easygoing dog has an equally laid-back owner. A nervous dog mirrors tension within the family.

Our dogs exhibit the effects of stress. They reflect erratic, hectic lifestyles and stressful environments in their behavior and with physical problems. Like their human owners, dogs can develop intestinal problems or nervous behaviors. Signs of stress in your dog are warning signals that you should heed for your own health, as well as your dog's. A simple thing like a long walk may alleviate stress for both of you.

This ability of dogs to act as mirrors is clearly seen in the story of Lisa, a teenage girl, and her German Shepherd, Mandi. Mandi was three years old and not housebroken, even though she had always lived indoors. As I talked with Lisa about this, she told me of the inconsistent and confusing attempts of her parents to housebreak the dog. Her father's idea of housebreaking was to hit Mandi when she relieved herself in the house. Lisa's mother felt sorry for the rough treatment Mandi received from her husband and tried to compensate by adopting a permissive attitude toward Mandi's accidents. To complicate the matter further, Lisa's mother had told her husband she didn't want him to hit the dog, so he only punished Mandi when his wife was not around.

Lisa realized that Mandi's housebreaking training was a reflection of her own upbringing. As a result of this inconsistent and confusing treatment, Mandi and Lisa had similar personalities; they were both timid, passive, and insecure. Using her dog as a mirror, Lisa was able to understand herself.

When Lisa's mother died, Lisa came to live with my husband and me. Mandi was placed in a loving home. She is now happy and housebroken. Lisa is a beautiful, confident young woman who now has her Animal Health Technician degree and received an award when she graduated for being the best all-around student in both academic and extracurricular activities. Positive reinforcement, consistency, and unconditional love worked wonders for both of them.

Unconditional Love

The greatest lesson dogs can teach us is unconditional love. This admirable trait was memorialized in a well-known speech given in 1869 as part of a closing argument in a court case involving the death of a dog.

> *The one absolutely unselfish friend that a man can have in this selfish world, the one that never deserts him and the one that never proves ungrateful or treacherous is his dog. . . . He will kiss the hand that has no food to offer, he will lick the wounds and sores that come in encounters with the roughness of the world. He guards the sleep of his pauper master as if he were a prince. When all other friends desert he remains. When riches take wings and reputation falls to pieces, he is as constant in his love as the sun in its journey through the heavens.*

People's craving for such love is undoubtedly why dog ownership is so popular. Dogs don't judge us. They don't care what we look like or how much money we make. They don't care if we say or do something stupid. The unconditional nature of their love is the reason dogs are such good therapists in nursing homes and with mentally disturbed people.

The example of unconditional love given to us by our dogs should be followed by us in our relationships with other humans. It is the kind of love that makes us feel that someone will love us no matter what we say or do. They may not like our actions, but they will always love us. It is love without conditions attached to it. Conditional love is the feeling that someone will stop loving you if you do not perform correctly or if you do not act as expected, such as a belief that your parents will stop loving you if you do not get good grades in school or that your husband will leave you if you argue with him.

We can provide others with the same sense of security, acceptance, and love that our dogs give us by giving them unconditional love. Children need it to grow into mentally healthy adults; marriages need it to be happy. It is the greatest gift your dog gives you; it is the best gift you can give to another.

Love to Grow On

Falling in love with a puppy is like failing in love with a human. It is the exciting beginning of a relationship, but it is only a temporary state. Reality soon sets in. With a puppy, reality is accidents on the rug, chewed shoes, and not coming when called. With a human, it is irritating habits and different priorities.

For the relationship to continue, whether it is with a dog or another person, this temporary love has to grow into real love. If it doesn't, the relationship ends. In humans, this often means a divorce. Unfortunately, dogs pay a

As the training goes, the love grows.

higher price when the love fails to grow. They are isolated in a cage in the backyard or abandoned at the local animal shelter to face probable death.

Real love is the act of extending yourself to help another achieve happiness. For it to develop, there has to be a commitment beyond keeping a dog or spouse as long as they make you happy. Realistic expectations, good communication, sensitivity, understanding, and unconditional love are all ingredients that contribute to its growth.

Training a dog should be an expression of real love. It should develop mutual communication and respect. It should not be done purely to meet your own needs, nor should it be done to dominate. Training is giving up something of yourself, your time and energy, to meet your dog's need for mental and physical exercise. It is striking the right balance between the necessity of exercising control for your dog's well-being and allowing him freedom to be a dog. As the training goes, the love grows. And so will you.

Index